THE ACCELERATED SELF

POWERFUL SOURCE GUIDANCE

TO

ENGAGE YOUR HIGHER SELF

FAST TRACK YOUR POTENTIAL

AND

WALK THE PATH OF GREATNESS

SONDRA SNEED

Source Communicator, Godscribe

DEDICATION

This work is for those who cry out
into the expanse looking for themselves
to find a greater being answering back.

ACKNOWLEDGMENTS

ONCE I DREAMED OF A DARK NIGHT'S SWIM. It's a mystery how I knew I was in France, but I was floating merrily down a stream, feeling refreshed by the cold of it. I watched my arms glide through the dark water, as I passed by houses that were brightly lit from within. When I drifted under a stone footbridge, I left the water and climbed the ravine to investigate. Blades of grass and mud oozed through my toes, as I scaled the embankment to find the bridge's foundation, which seemed miles high from where I started in the stream. Suddenly, the sky changed. In an instant, it went from a moonless, clear night below, to a bright overcast day on top, and it was snowing. I was admiring the quiet snowfall when a terrifying awareness began to grow inside me. Dense silence became overbearing. And then my attention turned to a snow-covered mountain, which grew to meet my gaze. I felt infinitesimal—small and unworthy. *This is God's place,* I thought to myself. *God lives here!* Cowering at the sight of the mountain's powerful forces, the bridge's guardrail I held onto became unstable. Like a mouse, I ducked, to hide behind the rock footing, feeling as if the bridge would break apart any moment. And that's when I woke-up, in a cold sweat.

I had that dream in my year of solitude over 20 years ago, when God first appeared through my pen. I have been climbing that immense mountain since. *The Accelerated Self* is a critical dimension of the ascent to master its power in my life and to bring that to others as a matter of purpose and mission.

Because not every climb is possible without help, I suck up my pride and ask for it. One bringer of aid is a brilliant student of *The Accelerated Self* program, editor and writer Samantha Dickinson. We first met when she had a soul reading with me at my booth during Contact in the Desert, an annual UFO conference. She dove straight into my work, and then stepped in to assist like an answered prayer. She's my editor for this book and I am grateful to work with a professional who is also an eager student. I would never have finished in less than a year without her intelligent absorption.

I also need to express gratitude for my previous publisher, Robert Friedman, who released my first book, *What to Do When You're Dead: A Former Atheist Interviews the Source of Infinite Being* in 2013, which is what led me into public work. Though his soul has crossed-over, I may not have had the courage otherwise. He published *Conversations with God* in 1995 by Neil Donald Walsh, which offered modern precedence in the field of communing with Universal Consciousness I call God. I wish Friedman were here now. His book mentoring is sorely missed.

As for my husband, Dee Brown, I thank God everyday. He grounds my sanity. He was raised by a spiritually devout mom, so he's comfortable with my mission and rarely questions it. He admires the many minds and souls my work touches. And because he knows God, he understands what drives me. But most of all, I am grateful for how he shows me the power a man has, to steady the wilds of a woman's soul.

I also want to thank another student, Kapil Tyagi, whose expertise in education platforms allows me practical confidence when building an expanding teaching program. His experience is an essential coach in the process.

My job as a teacher, consult, and facilitator for the voice of Universal Consciousness, would not have purpose without the many clients and students who find this work. On their behalf, I've broadened the library of knowledge and I am grateful for their dedication and humbling self-growth. I'm content knowing their minds expand, as mine does, and that they develop spiritually in our psychic therapy sessions. This book is for them, as well as for the many more who are ready for a new tale from the unseen realm, of which we are all a part.

Acknowledgments

CHAPTERS

INTRODUCTION

To set yourself up, before starting chapter one, document your immediate feelings. Describe how life *is*. Meaning, write about how you view the world and your place in it.

Are you angry, happy, sad, overwhelmed? And at what level of those feelings are you? Are they pervasive or intermittent? Are your feelings strong or bland? Do you carry the burden of the world on your shoulders, or have you become apathetic and uninterested? Does it seem that the world moves too fast? Or are you no longer keeping pace and just moving through life unengaged?

This book is going to change your perspective about yourself. So, when you review the chapters and then journal about what you've learned, you'll find out where the work will have the greatest impacts.

You will learn from this book the nine elements of self from the perspective of Universal Consciousness. This consciousness is referred to by the author as God, Source, and the Source of Infinite Being. But it is not limited to the author's access, because this higher consciousness is contained also within you.

The elements of self that are covered here-in, describe the aspects of individual consciousness as it relates to you. Not as it relates in general, but specifically to the one who recognizes its tenants.

This book cannot be consumed as a narrative, because the story of you is written in every moment of a new awareness. It is also not a how-to book, because the steps to integrate the ways and means of its truth are not verified by your experiences, but instead made whole in your conscious actions.

Therefore, what you're about to read will create more confusion in the thinking, at least until you apply what you're learning. Then, it's evident in your daily, reformed cognizance, which means simply the book makes sense to you when it is held against your beliefs, when it starts to tear down your original systems and build new foundations. That's when you know what you're reading has begun to process through your potential.

The goals you set in life have no meaning without purpose. But purpose has no context without the full actualization of the self. And therein lies the purpose of this book, to bring fundamental change in how you see yourself, and how you understand the capacity you have for greatness.

When what you do is done for the sake of your full fruition, everything you do performs better over time. With each reading of *The Accelerated Self*, you will bring awareness more and more to the hidden aspects of the self, and thereby expand your true potential, in accordance with the stronger, wiser, more confident version of you that shows up in the world.

No matter what it is you wish to be better at, as long as you engage the unseen aspects of you that we cover in this book, your experiences in life, past or present, no longer define what you can do. Instead, you begin to see your spirit raise, your soul enliven, and your mind become more illuminant.

With practice, your strength roots down into your more vulnerable places, instead of hidden. Your vulnerability hides to protect you from others. So, as that shifts, you become more honest in principle, and give others a reason to trust you and your intentions, which in turn, makes you a better leader.

As a leader, you draw more opportunities and vibrate with greater magnetism. You start to draw a better collection of influences, as well as more enlightened people to your circle of friends. You start to see the effect you have on others is more positive, offering you greater access to the circles you've been denied before. With a strong internal fortitude, you'll take smarter risks and feel more confident in your awareness of others. You'll make better judgments about who to enlist on your behalf.

You'll also notice the nuances that make up the unseen realm, to make you more intuitive and have a heightened awareness for what can go wrong and how to course correct in the small spaces on your life path, instead of having to clean up huge messes that come from an unhealthy karmic workload.

The shifts that begin to show up in joy and self-awareness help you become the person you were as a kid. You were once full of excitement over the small things life showed you. You can find that you once again.

Your accelerated self is not confined to the laws of your brain, but instead expands you into the likeness of your soul, and the power of your spirit. No two snowflakes are alike, but the truth is snow is not a snowflake. Nor is being human the same for every individual soul. So, finding the shape of your soul means giving form and shape to what makes you unique, special, and made by the Creator of all creatures, large and tiny.

Self-Discovery

Journal

CHAPTER ONE

THE WOUNDS

BLOOMING

Life is a foundation.

But there's also a foundation of life. And that foundation must come from some preexisting phenomena. Every preexisting phenomenon is the beginning of some other foundation.

Life begins in a foundation. That builds on another foundation. That devises another foundation. And each foundation that is built on top of itself eventually flowers into its full potential.

When you begin a process of a new awakening or a new awareness or a new you, it's always come from layers of foundations that you've built before the full fruition of you comes true. Once you reach that full fruition, you're ready to seed a new foundation.

And every new seed into a foundation is an amorphous experience. You get a sense of it. You get glimpses of it. But it has no shape. It has no form. On a certain day, you might see some reference to it, either in a person who's doing that thing you think you might want to do, or a reference to something that seems familiar, though you've never seen it before, or a reference that seems to be calling you, even though you've never been drawn to such a thing before.

Those glimpses start to open in bits and pieces, building that first foundation that comes from the seed, which sprouted from the last blooming that you've been blooming your whole life; in the sequence: foundation > foundation > foundation > bloom > seed > foundation > foundation > foundation > bloom > seed.

it's in every wound that you've experienced
a new foundation has bloomed

This chapter of the nine chapters of *The Accelerated Self* is called The Wounds. Though wounds are not the most exciting thing to talk about of which the universal construct could talk about, it is in fact the most foundational of all of the chapters, because it's in every wound that you've experienced in all of your life that a new foundation has bloomed.

Sometimes a wound will bloom a foundation that is protection. Sometimes a wound will bloom a foundation that is a redirection. *Oh, I will never be like my mother. I will never marry someone like my father.* These are foundations that are wounds that have generated new seeds.

And the problem with wounds, if there really is a problem—but we would say it's a problem that needs to be solved in your consciousness—the problem with wounds is that sometimes they don't allow you to know the difference between a foundation and a bloom, and you might think you're blooming in a relationship, for example, in the process of falling in love, only to find out that in the process of that relationship you have a wound. Deep, dark, difficult wound.

That flowering you experienced initially in the relationship has shown you the foundation you're standing on, from which you bloomed. And the foundation you're standing on may not be very solid. Because this wound that keeps coming up in this new blooming relationship is causing rifts in the relationship.

For some people, it's that one rift that causes them to flee. All it takes is that one little rift, and they're already heading out the door, even if they stay another four years, because that relationship comes back into the bloom. It feels like love. It feels like self. It feels like new. But actually it's a reminder of some weak point in the foundation.

CLOSING WOUNDS

If you look at wounds the way you would a gash or some kind of cut in the flesh, if it's wide enough, it's impossible for the skin to regrow the cells that create enough of a scar, in order that that wound is semi healed, or seemingly healed, because the scar is there to draw the skin closed.

But that is not a healing. It's a closure and a scar. If it's too wide and can't close, it will always be triggered. It's sore, it's open, it's unscarred, unclosed.

You have a lot of wounds that are not closed. In some cases, those open wounds are opportunities for growth. Little seeds drop into them, and you grow. You become very sensitive, and that sensitivity allows you to notice people in different ways.

You notice people who are in pain, and you want to comfort them, or you notice people who are angry, and you want to stay away from them. The only way you would know these conditions about them is if you too, have experienced some wound, and that reference point is the opening you still feel.

STANDING IT

But what about a wound that won't heal? It won't close, and it interrupts every relationship you're involved in. That kind of wound not only needs your attention, but it also needs foundation, to be a place you can stand. Otherwise, you can't stand. You can't stand it. *I can't stand people like that. I can't stand it when he does that. I can't stand it when she's so like that.* When you can't stand it, it means your foundation is interrupted from that wound. The issue is that every time you're in an experience you can't stand, it is a part of you that you can't stand. *I can't stand myself. I drive myself crazy.*

Rather than trying to heal those emotional disruptions of the self through meditation, healers, classes, psychologists, or psychics, instead of attempting to heal, first learn how to stand it.

As you can stand it, the wound starts to get a little bit closer. The edges move a bit closer and a bit closer. They move closer because the wound feels you loving it, trying to be more approachable to it.

Instead of can't stand it, which can manifest as, *I don't want to talk about it, that's more than I can handle.* Do this instead, *I'm going to try. I'm going to stand right here, and*

I'm going to feel that. I'm just going to feel all the things I can't stand to feel, and as I feel it... as I feel more okay... I'm just going to feel it.

The more you allow yourself to *feel* it, those are the edges of the wound coming closer to each other, instead of recoiling away, festering, and waiting for your attention.

SCARS

Scars are not healings. The scar is not the healed-over perfect skin. Scars are the healed you attempting to close a wound. So, coming from a healed space, standing in a wound draws it closer. You're healing it from a whole place. Though the scar will remain, it reminds you that it's there. It will also show you how hard you worked to close that wound.

SCARS, BOUNDARIES, AND WALLS

What's the difference between a closed wound and a closed energy? Or a closed mind? Or maybe an emotional wall? Because they're all barriers you close to avoid more wounding. But if it's closed off and no one can enter in, then it's the healed you that doesn't get a chance to be. The healed you doesn't get a chance to be among. And for people who are sensitives, this is a very dangerous place to be, to be walled-off in a fortress. The wound is within and it's inside the you that is healed. If you stand in the wound that needs your attention, and you don't give it anxiety or a tension that says,

I've got to heal this. If I don't get this healed, I know I won't be easy to be around. People will always say I'm too much. I'm just too much. Somehow, I must heal this.

To open and not close yourself off from others, first remove from your mind the intense pressure to heal.

We're not saying you should open your boundaries, because you need to protect your spirit. Your spirit must be protected, and boundaries are critical for that. Especially if you have wounds that you have yet to understand, then you may call-in the wounded if you don't have proper boundaries. We suggest opening just enough however, to create a permeable boundary.

Permeable boundaries allow you to control what comes in and what goes out, without demanding all out. This permeability removes the pressure to maintain strict control over what's going on inside you, or demand control over what's going on outside you.

What you must control instead is the border. *You can come in, and you can't. You need to leave and not come back. You are here for a reason, and your reason is unknown to me, but I see you, I know you. And the way you're making me feel right now makes me unsure of you. Here are the places in me that I think you might wound me. I just want you to know I'm watching you.* You are a guard at the gate.

Now, let's look at wounds as a condition of the gate.

THE GUARDIAN

Once upon a time, in a land far away, there was a guardian that had nowhere to stay.

This guardian would hover around, attempting to find a place to land, but couldn't find anywhere that wanted this guardian around. Because this guardian had a lot of rules.

It had rules for in and rules for out, and all those rules meant control. As that guardian hovered looking for a place to land, a friendly place to be, all it heard was, *Back away! Get back! You're in my stuff. This is my stuff. Get out of here. Go away. I don't need you. I can do it myself. I got this. You just move on.*

And everywhere that guardian saw this kind of behavior, it realized, *No one wants me, no one needs me. I have no job. There's nothing for me to do here. I have no home.* And that is a part of you. It's the guardian in you with no home.

When you think you've got it handled, you can figure it out, and you don't need anyone to help you, it's the condition in you that's warding off your guardian, the guardian you are.

How do you know you are a guardian? How do you know there's a guardian in you? Every time you try to control a situation that is difficult or impossible to control. That is the guardian in you attempting to be, attempting to take control and protect the situation.

But how do you know the difference between a situation that doesn't need you, and a situation that welcomes you as a guardian? Think about that for a moment: the thing in you that doesn't need you, and the thing in you that is the guardian. The thing in you that is a guardian is the part in your heart that had to survive a wound all by yourself.

That part had no one to comfort you, no one to take care of you and make sure you were okay. The one thing or two things or three things, major points in your life where you alone had to care.

That's the part in you that needs the guardian and wards off the guardian. *I got this handled. I figured this out a long time ago, long before you ever came around, long before I ever knew you were even here. I got this all figured out. I'm good.*

But it's not until you're in an argument, either with yourself or someone else, that it's very clear it isn't handled. For the wounding, you need a guardian. You need someone protecting you, because this person you're arguing with is somehow reflecting that wound and you are geared up for a fight.

WOUNDS THAT DON'T FIGHT

Some people have wounds that don't fight. They just fall over, belly up and say, *Go ahead. It's happened to me many other times. Happens all the time. Go ahead. Take my power. Take my energy. Take my joy.*

That's the part of you that needs the guardian the most, you that's used to it, who's used to the taking.

So how do you get that wound to stand up, to have some foundation so that you can stand in the course of your own need? How do you get a wound to stand up for your need? *Look, I need you to back off. I need you to pay the bill. I need you to remember that what I do is valuable. I need you to remember what I am that is valuable.*

This is your guardian standing up for you, not letting you lie down and take it.

There are some people in this world who are guardians by nature. These people are usually the most controlling, too. They are, in some regards, control freaks and they can't help it. Because they are protectors. That's their job. So, they control everything. And then other people just let them control everything, because there would be a fight if they had to stand up to that.

But the truth is, protectors don't know they're being controlling any more than an English sheep dog knows that it's being controlling. It's doing its job. That's what it's there for. Its job is to herd everybody in a circle and to move along. That's their job.

If you have relationships with controllers, or if you are a controller, know that it comes from a nature to protect.

But you do not need to lay low or lay down, belly up, and let them control your stuff. And you also don't have to put up a wall, so they don't. Instead, you can say, *Hey, this is my job. That's your job. Thank you, but this part's my job.*

When it comes to taking care of you though, maybe you say, *Thank you for taking care of me today. Thank you for doing what I could not do by myself. Thank you for being there when I couldn't be there for myself.*

VULNERABILITY AND BELONGING

Allowing someone to care for you takes a lot of vulnerability. It takes you being vulnerable enough to let down your guard enough so someone can be there for you. The reason you may not be good at letting someone take care of you is because of all those wounds you had to deal with all by yourself, without anyone there. But that vulnerability means permeability.

It means recognizing where you need to protect what is important to you, and then recognizing when it's really not that important to you to take care of yourself right now. Sometimes it's important so that you can move on to care for others, to let someone take care of you right now. If you just go around saying, *I'm fine,* every time someone offers a hand, it becomes a habit. And you never demonstrate your vulnerability, you never offer anyone an opportunity to care.

So how do you get to that place?

HOW DO YOU GET TO VULNERABLE?

Think of a baby just being born into the hands of a doctor, the hands of nurses, passed around. That baby doesn't know what is going on. It can't do anything but cry. It has no sense of these cold hands, this bright light in a room. All it knows is it's uncomfortable. And then when it's all cleaned up and bundled, and placed in the hands of its mother, suddenly this child recognizes where it belongs. That's when belonging begins.

But imagine if that child at some point in the relationship has a separation from that belonging, that's vulnerability.

And it's at that separation point, you either must fend for yourself or die. Sometimes the separation is figurative because separation literally happens later in life. But fending for yourself or die is built into the structure of nature. And nature is constantly finding ways to make babies less vulnerable. Whether you're a tiny baby literally, or a newborn spiritually, nature's always trying to find a way to make that infant less vulnerable.

spiritual infancy... when you
just start to understand
that there's more to you than this physical body

Imagine, in the way we just described, what vulnerability is but consider spiritual infancy. It's when you just start to understand that there's more to you than this physical body. That's when the separation starts to occur between the body and spirit to create delineation.

Just like the baby is separated from the mother or the belonging, the body is suddenly no longer the totality of you, and the spirit starts to rise and show itself. If you don't see belonging in that spirit and nurture that sense of belonging of spirit, the vulnerability from the loss of that belonging becomes a constant state of wounding.

Because of your separation, you get vulnerable and sensitive around people when you awaken spiritually. You'll want to try to control your environment, so that you're only around spiritual people, only around people who will understand you spiritually. Because when you're around people who don't have a spiritual life in any way, as you start to open your mouth about vibrations and chakras, they give you a smirk and roll their eyes.

Then you lose that feeling of belonging with your own family and longtime friends. In lost belonging, the real world looks harsh. This causes some to quit their jobs and join an ashram in India, just to be surrounded by spiritual people, so they don't have to face the cold world.

But when they return home to be around their family and other people, out in the world again, they want to run right back because they are ill prepared. Their wounds are bare, completely exposed to a hard reality, a harsh cruel world.

HOW NOT TO LOSE YOURSELF TO THE WORLD

If you have a role to play in the world, guided from your spiritual nature, you've got to find a way to both protect yourself and not lose yourself. Which is why you have an urge to protect yourself in the first place, so you don't lose yourself again, back into the world, as you spiritually awaken.

Remember the place of permeability. Be a guardian at the gate. Because if you remain faithful to your awakening spirit, the world will show you what you've won, as a strong spiritual nature.

Here's one way to do that. Because not all your wounds get healed simply because you're spiritually aware, channeled, and tuned in. Those wounds do not just naturally heal. So, to reduce the effect of the hard, cruel world against that new spiritual belonging, what you're going to learn today is how to rake across a wound as it attempts to scar.

RAKING THE SCARRING

Your wounds naturally contain attempts to scar within them. Just as blood coagulates when the skin is cut, a psychological wound's attempt to scar is what distorts parts of the body, like your fascia, or even shapes the way of your walk. It's why parts of your body hold a great deal of tension; where you attempt to close the wound.

Loosening the fibers of a wound in your psyche, by mentally raking through it, diminishes the distortion of being all held up in your muscles and joints.

It's important to practice because when someone triggers your wounds, all that tension you are using to hold wounds closed will become all the tension you put into your dialog with them. Or all the tension you hold, after a conversation that shows you how much they don't agree with you.

And not only do they not agree with you, maybe they're changing their opinion of you because of that conversation. Imagine all the fear that creates, all that separation from belonging. When you get into a conversation like that with someone who doesn't believe what you believe, someone who doesn't care about what you care about, and that fear that you don't belong anymore because of it—you're going to take all that feeling and you're going to rake it, using an imaginary wooden comb.

you don't have to feel belonging from the ones
who make you feel separation

Picture big gaps between each of the teeth of that wooden comb. Imagine it firmly raking the fibrous wound of separation. The reason wood is important to this self-soothing technique is because wood has a natural sound. It has a natural wave vibration. It has its own timbre. As its raked across the texture of fibers that come from the attempt to scar, the imaginary wooden sound creates a wave, a vibrational pattern that restructures the wound. That wave provides a feeling of release of tension around the wound, allowing closure and relief.

BELONGING

You don't have to feel belonging from the ones who make you feel separation. All you need is to not be reminded of the times you had to deal with all those wounds all by yourself. Because that's what those conversations remind you of.

You're reminded of the harsh cruel world out there, no longer in here; no longer in mother's womb and fully protected, but out there. All the reminders of being out there has wound after wound, after wound, after wound. Wounds that come from your siblings or recess in school. Wounds going from sixth grade to junior high. Big wounds in seventh grade. To high school! Lots of wounds in high school. To finally being mature enough, only to find you're inadequate because the big adult world expects something from you that you don't have.

More wounds, more separation, no more belonging.

Every time you've had to find some sense of independence in the world, whether it's from relationship to relationship, job to job, security to insecurity, these are all wounds that constantly remind you of the first separation.

THE THOUGHTS YOU KEEP

We're going to take this idea further now. Moving deeper into what we've discussed so far, as the external wounds from events in your life, to going into the deeper levels of wounding, which come from you.

You wound yourself in your thoughts and by the thoughts you keep.

Thoughts are programs in the brain. They are not in the mind. The mind is the processor of all. But the brain is the keeper of thoughts. The brain keeps memories and the turbulence or joy connected to memory.

Thoughts the brain keeps run programs from all of the wounds you've ever experienced. They're all in there. And whether you remember the actual experience that the thought held, you revisit it repeatedly when you feel hurt. And sadly, it's you who is the biggest injurer of yourself there is, because these programs run until you turn them off.

They loop until your greater mind says, *Hey, let's go do something. Maybe we just get up and go do the dishes or something.*

The greater mind has the capacity to look at those thoughts and not feel anything from them. The body, however, is not so lucky.

THE BODY REMEMBERS

The body contorts with every thought it revisits that injures. It contorts because it's listening to a warped thought on a loop, a loop with no end. And the reason these thoughts wind up in loops is because they have no conclusion. There's no conclusion because the brain is looking for the truth.

The brain tries to find the truth, and since there's no truth in those thoughts, the brain loops, looking for truth. If at some point, somewhere, somehow, someone, or something tells you the truth about those thoughts, they'll release. They'll stop looping.

But some thoughts carry no truth, and there's nothing anyone could say that will ever release you from that thought. Because it's old. It's an old thought that was programmed before you even knew how to experience an experience as a child. You just took on experiences as they came, before you knew how to process an experience. You're jerked around by the experience.

WHAT IS TRUE?

We are looking for truth in these thoughts, but let's now think about what truth is.

Some people think truth is individual. They believe everybody has their own truth. But we say that's impossible. It can't be true if everyone has some version of it, there's no way for it to be true.

True is true, no matter what.

Someone may have a different experience, or a different perspective, but they don't have a different truth. They might have a different set of circumstances that brought them to a conclusion that then became an opinion and that opinion became a habit—but it's not a truth. It's not a true.

That's why people cannot release a truth for you, you've got to recognize that it is true—for it to be true—and then it releases the brain that has a loop on a thought.

Let's say you and a sibling, who is someone with similar experiences growing up, such as you and your brother or sister, and you argue about an experience. It's the same experience. You both went through it, and you argue about it. What does that say about truth?

It says that the experience effected each brain in perspective differently. Same experience. But you're arguing about what happened or whose fault it was. It's a different perspective of the event.

The same is true about a wound.

So, if you can find a perspective that is true, such as, *you're worth more than that. You keep thinking that and you'll never know your value.* That's true. *You can't find any value by thinking that thought. You'll die with that thought.* That's true.

THOUGHTS THAT KILL

You can die from thought. You die inside emotionally, die from heartache, die from unresolved issues wherein you cannot find the truth, and you die a little at a time.

But how do you fix that wound that will not close? And it triggers every time you fall in love. That's how we end this chapter. We're going to end on, *How do you manage a wound that will not resolve?* Because you'd have to kill off people in order for it to resolve; it's either you or them.

HOW TO RESOLVE A THOUGHT LOOP

Begin with the truth.

The truth is:

> *If I keep thinking about this today, I will wind up in bed.* Truth.

Second truth:

> *There is nothing I can do about this. This is beyond me. God, please take this from me.*

Truth number three:

> *God, if it's meant for me to find a better way to deal with this, please bring it to me.*

Truth number four:

> *God, I know I have to visit you with this all the time, but it keeps flooding back. I keep getting reminded. And it's hurting me, and I don't know how to get over it.*

Truth number five:

> *God, I know I came to you with this yesterday, and you took it off me and off my heart for a little while, and you got me through the day. Thank you for that. Thank you for getting me through the day. But I felt it come back today. I felt it come back today, and it came back hard. It came back really hard. Please take it from me today. Please allow me to sleep a good sleep.*

These are the prayers of truth.

Your true spiritual self encourages blooms, even in an environment that doesn't look like it can bloom

Maybe they're about a wound you can't solve because that means other people must be different. They must either heal from addiction, or they have to like you or love you, and they don't like you or love you; and you can't change that.

The only one who can change that is the greater mind above your thoughts, the greater way above your way, the foundation under your foundations, the bloomer of your blooms, the seed of your seeds.

It is the origin of your true nature, your true being, your true spiritual self, which encourages those blooms, in an environment that doesn't look like it can bloom, and an environment that has people who are harsh and hard. That's the opportunity in the truth, no matter what.

Self-Discovery – Chapter 1 – The Wounds

1.   **What is the condition for truth?**

    a.   recognizing true is true no matter what

    b.   when you let go of your opinion

    c.   resolve: it completes the quest for truth

    d.   when everyone agrees with what the truth is

2.   **What is the absence of truth?**

    a.   separation

    b.   different opinions

    c.   an incomplete perspective

3.   **Why do people get lost?**

    a.   because they hide from the world

    c.   because they hide from the truth

    d.   because they separate from belonging

4.   **Where is a dependable source of belonging?**

    a.   your parents: because they will always love you no matter what

    b.   spirit: because it is a return to oneself

    c.   yourself: because you can't separate from yourself

5. **From where does the world 'out there' enter the psyche?**

    a.   through your emotional attachments

    b.   through your brain, your thoughts

    c.   through your actions

6. **Why do wounds matter?**

    a.   because we learn

    b.   because they form our foundations

    c.   because they shape our decisions and to master our wounds is to master our decisions

    d.   all of the above

7. **What's the difference between a closed wound and a closed energy?**

    a.   one is a scar, the other a wall

    b.   a wound is closed from a healed place; energy is closed because of an open wound

    c.   a closed wound has been attended to, taken care of; closed energy is an ignored wound

    d.   all of the above

Journal Prompt – Get inspired!

Write about times in your life when your achievements have bloomed from a kernel of thought:

---

every new seed into a foundation
is an amorphous experience

Amorphous means without form or shape. Where do you think these amorphous experiences are most likely to take place? How did they end up shaping you? Take a moment to scan your accomplishments. What preceded them?

The clearest way to identify this idea is in the moments of inspiration. Long before any action was taken.

Answers: 1c, 2a, 3c, 4b, 5b, 6d, 7d

Self-Discovery

Journal

Self-Discovery

Journal

CHAPTER TWO

THE MIND

IN A LAND FAR AWAY

A long time ago, there was once an itty-bitty, teeny-tiny mollusk. This little mollusk had only one job. Its job was to maintain water temperature.

Now the water temperature it was to maintain was just what was around the little mollusk. Not the whole water temperature in all of the ocean, but the water temperature nearby. And it maintained this water temperature very simply, by breathing in and breathing out. It would breathe in the cool water and breathe out warm water.

As it breathed in the cool water around it, the mollusk could feel that cool water cooling its little body, and it would warm that water as it breathed it back out. That's all it did.

Breathing in and out was its only job. There was nothing else the small being needed to do or needed to be. But this mollusk had no idea that this one job that it had to do was all that it mattered to do. It thought maybe it was supposed to do something else.

That was too easy. It's too easy, it would say. *All I must do is breathe in and breathe out, and something changes. And that's the whole of it. Surely there's something more to it, surely there's something more to my life. Why was I born? Why was I made here? Why am I even here?*

Little did it know that its very special design would eventually proliferate to warm the waters, in such a degree that it would create an environment for something else to grow, something else to populate. Because the temperature was too cold for that thing that needed to populate. And that thing that needed to populate, as it populated, would become food for something else. And then that something else that would eat the food, was also food; and to be food, its only job was to continue to eat.

Now the mollusk couldn't see this prolonged chain of reaction. It had no idea that the ease of its work every day was all that was necessary. And so it fretted, every day, wondering if it was enough. *Am I doing enough? Am I being enough? Is there something else I'm supposed to be?*

THE MIND

This mollusk represents the nature of the mind and how the mind works. The mind has a very simple task. Its task is simply to process perception. That perception is processed in a way that feeds other conditions of the mind. Those conditions of the mind, which are fed by the mind, are replicated *in* the mind, so that consciousness has a way of being, by feeding other aspects of itself.

When it comes to an individual mind, it is contained in a much larger mind. Just as the mollusk is a tiny little mind, it's contained in a bigger, and a bigger, and a bigger, and a bigger mind. Every role that this tiny little mollusk plays will play another role.

Each consecutive role advances the condition of that mollusk by building an environment and an ecosystem that comes back and feeds the mollusk. The same is true of the mind.

When the environment and the ecosystem of the mind is full, full of the rich abundant essence of its own processing, that means every part of that mind is being fulfilled. This mind of fulfillment is a mind with a capital M—Mind. This means fulfillment is not the little mind with one job, but the greater mind that is processing all jobs of all its small minds. That greater mind was once a tiny little mind with one job, to breathe in and breathe out, to bring in and bring out. But the more this mind made of itself as it was breathing, the more it could observe.

The more this mind observed, the greater that mind became. Because of its observations and its processes, the processes of that mind became the observations *in* the mind.

---

every tiny bit of information it
is able to process
builds an environment around the brain

THE BRAIN IS NOT THE MIND

The mind is not just a condition of the brain. The brain is simply an organ designed to bring organization to the mind. The brain has neurological pathways that are designed by programming from its environment, such that the brain knows how to perceive what's going on around it.

Because of the brain, the bigger process of the mind knows the difference between a friend and a foe, a mother and a father, a sibling and a stranger, and these neurological pathways are being programmed from the tiniest mental stimulation. That brain is processing, *Who is that? I know that person. That person comes around every day. I know what's in that bowl, I know that that is a bowl which is different than a plate.*

Every tiny bit of information its is able to process builds an environment around it, around a brain that's processing the mind. This brain processing the mind builds up all kinds of memories. But those memories are also associating with physical function.

That brain has to know how to walk, how to talk, how to interact, how to draw, use, and interpret language. That's the purpose of the brain. But it's not the purpose of the mind.

The mind is the curiosity of what is said, or what's over there, or what is the foundation I'm standing on. This is where we're going concerning the condition of the mind. Because the mind is a huge topic, on which we can only scratch the surface in a single chapter. To tell you a little bit about what its job is, what it's related to, and the course that the mind takes throughout your life, we'll discuss how your mind tends to grow and then it deflates.

THE MIND GROWS AND DEFLATES

With every deflation in a growth, there is compaction from the growth. That deflation feels like depression, but it is not. It is compaction, organization, re-interpretation. Only the mind, not the brain, can control interpretation.

The brain only knows its memory, its programming, what's been given to it, what it's breathed in, and all that condition of its breathing in. But it doesn't know the condition of breathing out, letting go, receiving and doing something with what has been received. Doing something with what the brain has received is a function of the greater mind in you.

THE GREATER THE MIND WITHIN

When you have properly programmed the greater mind in you, it's based on the curiosity you have about your own mind. This makes the both the compaction and organization periods creative.

The mind creates from the point of compaction and organization. Often the most creative periods in your life have been when no one was around to interrupt you. No one was around to tell you how to do something. You did it based on will, the will to see what would happen *if*. Or the question, *What's over there?*

The mind has an ability to take all that organization and compaction and then reinterpret it. The brain is just storing the information, warehousing it, and it gets full, making it really hard to manage. Which is why those periods of compaction that feel like depression are really important to the creation of the mind that you are. And the process is simple.

Although the process of the creation of the mind you are is simple, just like the mollusk, if you're constantly asking what you should be that is more than what you are, you'll never get a glimpse into the real creative potential.

THE CREATIVE POTENTIAL OF THE GREATER MIND

The creative potential in the mind is the most overlooked part of individual processing. It's not overlooked when you compare yourself to other people, unfortunately, because you'll see the creative processing in them and feel stagnant by comparison.

You'll always feel inadequate by comparison unless you give the creative processing in you room to be. The space may mean you allow yourself to be really bad at something brand new.

The mind needs to give you freedom, and the only way it gives you that autonomy is when you see yourself as that mollusk asking questions about what it's doing.

- *Why am I here?* Keeps you on task.

- *What am I doing?* Reminds you where you are.

- *Why is this so important?* Helps you remember the rules of engaging your task.

- *This seems so simple. I do this so easily. It's second nature.* Tells you who you are.

- *It can't be important.* Questions your reasons.

The reason some things seem second nature is because the greater mind that you are, has already been given to you. It's given to this lifetime, in this wave of your being, but you have to explore that ease in everything you do.

progress is only visible when you
notice how far you've come
not how far you have to go

So, if you change the environment based on what's coming into you, in such a way that what comes out of you seems inadequate, you're not seeing the bigger picture of the impact. You're not seeing where it's going, why it's an important part of the cycles of your progression and your growth. Because the progression of your growth can seem so tedious when all you're doing is questioning the things that come so easily for you.

The things that come so easily for you make difficult new things possible. It's because of the stair-step condition of the mind. *I know how to do this. I do this well. This is the first place I go before I try this new thing. This new thing looks hard. But this where I am is easy. I want to be able to do this new thing. This easy thing can't possibly be all that I am. This here, in the middle of where I'm headed from where I've been, it doesn't seem like it is enough, like I'm enough.*

The middle of your stair-step mind appears as if you're inadequate because you're only halfway there. You can't see where you are in the process. The progress is only visible when you notice how far you've come, not how far you have to go.

The mind must have its process, which goes like this: compaction, reflection, expansion, compression, reflection, expansion. When you have these periods of reflection in the stair-step of the mind, you're able to determine if what you've done so far is even insular to where you're going. Meaning, *is it even in you to do what you're wanting to do?*

When you reflect on the mind's compaction, what do you have to know? What do you need the reflection to tell you? You'll need to know what the brain's memorized and mastered, right? You must have knowledge already learned in the brain, or you'll repeat your steps until they are learned.

This means that what you've accomplished so far needs an internal process. It's insular to you. The mind must already take you there. It needs to take you to where you are going to next. Right here, where you are, from the lower places in the process of the mind are incomplete reflections of where you're headed. But here is also where your wishes are, where your true self resides, because the true self is always expanding from right here.

COMPRESSION AND EXPANSION

Expansion and compression are simultaneous in the mind. Compression eliminates all the parts, or all the parts of the parts of you, that are unessential to expansion. Mistakes, wrong turns, and incompletions are fluff and vapor. Compaction and reflection get you down to the essential of what you're best at. They will take you back to the fundamentals.

[Hello dear reader, it's Sondra here, interupting Source to share a recent example that illustrates compaction and reflection. When God told me to convert "The Accelerated Self" program, into a book and workbook, and then audiobook, my brain whirred like a milk frother considering the hundreds of steps to accomplish that. The future was so distracting in fact, I spent a week just editing chapter one of the recorded content. But then, something unthinkable happened. I accendently deleted the Word Doc I was editing. Poophhhf! I blinked and it was gone. How do you recover a week's work? Well, how else? You start over. But guess what? It only took a few hours. Seven days were compressed into hours. Why? I'm sure you can guess. When the mental noise around the project fell silent. As panic and frustration sharpened my awareness of the task at hand, I zeroed-in on the essential. Compaction. I wonder now what your examples might be. What's a good story of how you eliminated the un-essential? Jot down anything that comes to mind. Now, back to the training.]

THE KNOW-NOTHING STAGE

Returning to the fundamentals allows the mind to build from your true self.

As a comparison, let's look at the alternative to pairing down to basics. What happens when you try to skip the first steps of a stair-step mind?

Let's say you want to learn how to paint. In the way you want to learn how to paint, you have no idea how to use a brush, what the different brushes are, how to use acrylic paint, how to choose colors, and how to mix colors. You have no idea how to build color on top of itself, to build a picture.

So, if you put paint on a brush, onto a canvas, and you try to draw some lines with that brush, you'll do little more than what you'd do with a pen, right? Where you begin, in the know-nothing stage of the thing you want to learn how to be in the mind, requires a mastery of some kind. In this case, your mastery is not painting. You must admit you know nothing, before you put paint to a canvas.

But what if you've already tried it that way and gave up by deciding it looks too hard. You couldn't do it naturally. *Well, I'm not natural at this, so it must not be my thing. I must not be able to do this ultimately.* That's the usual approach people take to something new and hard, at work, or relationships, or hobbies, or parenting.

Your approach to a new thing must begin in the investigation. The research in our example starts with a video of someone painting. You observe all the master's processes to make paint on a canvas look like something. To stay the course, we suggest you start from what you're already good at.

You're probably good at learning. It's something you learned how to do when you were very small. You learned how to learn. This is the condition of the mind that's filling itself up with cool water. It's breathing in. It's about getting information and learning, but before you can breathe out, the mind must know the fundamentals, for your effort to have some predictable effect.

Maybe you're good at color. Let's say color is something you already know how to do. You do it in your living room, in your bedroom, on your walls, or in your clothing style. You're just good at color. And you're good at picking colors.

So, start there. *What is it I need to learn about color mixing so I can make a color from two primary colors? And what of each of these primary colors is going to make the color I'm trying to recreate?* Like a seafoam green or a silver white at the top of an ocean wave, or a blue that seems to have many blues, and clouds that seem to have many grays.

This is the first thing you look at before you put paint onto a brush onto a canvas. Because even if you can't draw to save your life, you are at least investing in the way of making color, so that what you put on that canvas is predictable.

When you can predict what's going on the canvas and how you get there, the mind then, in this relationship, has recorded the condition of color from a tendency to love color. The mind is the tendency to love color. But the brain processes the primary colors, and that when added together will make another color. The brain is training and learning this process. The mind, however, knows there's a difference between a blue that is high in the sky and a blue that means the sun is low in the sky, because the mind looks for those differences.

MAKING MONEY

Someone might think as they're reading this, *I don't care about painting, I don't care about colors. I want to know how to make money. I am poor, and I'm sick of being poor, and I want to make money. And the reason I got this book,* The Accelerated Self, *is because I thought it was going to help me make money, because it's going to help me be better at the things that I'm not good at. I want to make money!*

But if you have never been good at making money, you cannot begin with money as the reason for expanding your consciousness. Just as you can't begin to learn painting by putting it on your brush and smearing it on a canvas. It must begin where you are with a love of learning or love of color.

You must look at, *What is it that makes money that I can do?* And begin there. Begin where you are, and expand from where you are, and then learn *at* that place. Then the stair-step becomes less tiresome, and you don't wear out before you reach your goal. *It can't be this. It's too easy. I do this all the time. I've done this my whole life.*

The condition of the mind must be that what you are breathing in is your learning. What you are expressing out has been processed through you. What you put out has already been processed by what's already in you. It cannot be processed by something you've never looked at or you've never considered. It's never been an option before because the mind is difficult to scale.

SCALING THE MIND

Let's look at how the mind is scaled. How do people go from growing up in poverty to becoming rich entrepreneurs? Often that poverty forced them into finding very creative ways to make money, creative ways to get food on the table, clothes on their back, and shoes on their feet. All that creativity to make that money is what made them an entrepreneurial mind.

From their industrious mind, they discovered something about the world at large that would offer them a greater scale of financial benefit. Whether it was buying at one price then selling at a higher price, or acquiring a skill that people need and being able to do it better than anyone else can do it. They build customers and clients, and they get better at that.

Once that entrepreneur mind mastered getting customers, they learned how to be a leader. From a leader they train others, and those others bring money back to the entrepreneur. But they always begin somewhere from where they began.

Where did you begin? Where did you experience your life?

Now, if you experienced your life in a place that if you replicate what you saw, you would either get fired or thrown in jail, if that is the condition that you are driving yourself out of, then the thing you must learn is that someone else's mind has been programmed with things you need to learn. There is always someone willing to teach and teach you outside of your area of outlook.

THE MIND IN A DEPRESSED STATE

Let's look now at how the mind works when you're stuck in a dark corner, when you're in a state of depression. The mind can be a terrible thing when it enters the brain, and then starts to process bad memories, bad experiences, and relives them over and over, again. In those times, it's not the mind at work at all, although people think it is.

People will say, *How do I turn my mind off? How do I turn my mind off so I can sleep, so I can think, so I can function?*

The truth is that you want the opposite to occur. You want to turn the mind on.

You want to turn the thoughts off and turn the mind on. The mind must stop processing through thought. You want the mind to process instead through task. By putting the mind on a task instead of your thoughts, it's processing the task, not the thought. Depression is always the mind being processed through thoughts and filtered through darker thoughts.

Let's look at that little mollusk again. What has it learned? If it's learned a lot of bad information or drawn in a lot of bad water, it's filtering that muck when it breathes out. It's having to filter through that bad water to make good warm water. When it must filter all through bad water, it's not breathing in very well. It's also not learning, and it's not breathing out very well. Therefore, it's not warming; it's not doing its job.

CLEAN THE FILTER

The filter and the water are two very important parts of understanding the mind. The filter is the brain, the water is the mind. The filter gets clogged with thoughts you think. If you are aware or can learn what those thoughts are and wash them away with clean mind, then what's filtered back out has been cleaned by the mind, and all those little particles that are clogging up that filter can be washed out with just a clean mind. A clean mind comes from things like exercise.

Exercise can be as simple as breathing clean air, sitting in meditation, and breathing clean air to exercise your lungs. Or it can be something as simple as gardening or walking. Because here's how thoughts work.

Thoughts are in the brain as memories. When the mind is filtered through those memories, the thoughts wake up. They're alive again. When the mind forgets those memories, they are down and buried. They are buried in other thoughts, new thoughts, clean thoughts, good thoughts. But the minute you start to filter that mind back through those memories, those dark thoughts will remerge, and when they do, they are just as fresh and new as the moment they were made. Those memories never go away. Unless you forget them, bury them.

Now, there may be times in your life where you get reminded, and you start digging up your own grave. But the mind is your friend in those times, also. When you listen to the mind, the greater mind, the mind that is above and beyond the small mind, when you listen to the greater mind, it will say to you, *Don't listen to that thought. Don't think about those thoughts. Those thoughts are very dark.*

But I don't know what to do with those thoughts. They hurt me.

There's only one way to manage those dark thoughts, and that's to replace them. *But I'm told I'm supposed to think about that; that I'm supposed to fix it somehow. And every time I think about it, my heart breaks. My world is upside down, and I can't do anything about it.* It's possible the thought you're thinking about, the thing you're supposed to think, is intertwined with darkness. It's not that the thought itself is dark. It's that it's intertwined with dark thoughts.

The mind of the greater mind comes in and looks at those thoughts. It unpacks them one by one. The greater mind can see that this isn't just one thought after all. It's a whole bunch of thoughts jumbled in there. For example, the way you think about your father and how he thinks about you may be related to some ex-boyfriend over here, or some cruel thing a girl said to you a long time ago when you were weak and sad and tired. All these other things start coming out as you start to unpack thoughts.

The mind is indifferent. The mind doesn't really notice whether this is a cruel thought, a bad thought, a dark thought. All the mind knows is that these are thoughts. *I see these thoughts. I see that thought and that thought and that thought and that thought, and how interesting those thoughts connect.* When the mind is at work, instead of the brain, the filter is no longer obsessed with the thought. It's obsessed instead with reflection, a reflection on the self.

The accelerated self is not a fully cleaned-out filter that's now pristine, new, and healed. Your accelerated self observes those thoughts and recognizes where they belong. Do they belong buried, never to be looked at again? Are they things you cannot change? Are they things that will never change? Things that every time you try to change only causes more problems? Those are the thoughts that must stay buried.

The accelerated self is also a mind that looks at thoughts or the conditions of thoughts you *can* change. Can you approach yourself a little more friendly, more kind, reassuring yourself that all the agony that has come at you, through all that muddied water you were filtering, all that agony was not *you?* It's someone else. It's something else. It came from out *there*. It belongs out there. Let's wash it out. That's where it belongs. The mind will change the location of thoughts when you give the mind a moment to observe those thoughts without emotion.

EMOTION AND THOUGHTS

Emotion is irritation. It's not feeling. We're not talking about feeling because emotion is what the body does as it responds to a feeling. The body emotes. It shouts, it cries, or it laughs. These effects are irritations that come from feelings, but they are not feelings. Have you ever noticed how you might laugh when you're nervous? That kind of laugh is an irritation emoting from nervousness; from not knowing what to do with your nervousness.

All these irritations get trapped in the filter, which causes the body to erupt in a response. Imagine little, feeler fingers waving through water as the mind processes a thought. In that filter is an irritated wound and it triggers an emotion. Something processing through your system may be innocent, totally neutral, but because it hits that irritation, it can cause a laugh, a tear, or a tension.

Maybe your friend says something you blow out of proportion, for example. You don't know why you lost your composure, and you're sorry later. *I don't know why I saw it that way. It's not like you at all to say something like that anyway. I don't know why I responded to you that way.* Your explosive reaction is probably related to a thought you need to unpack.

The more you're able to untangle those intertwined thoughts, the quicker you can get to the source of your out-of-whack reactions. That's self-awareness. And until you get good at self-awareness, an emotional reaction is on the same loop as the thought that put it there.

But let's look even deeper at the mind that processes these thoughts in the brain. Just as a wound becomes a hidden irritation in the processor, distorting feelings into unpredictable emotions, the mind also interrupts itself and can take you off course at any turn.

THE MIND INTERRUPTS

The mind interrupts itself, as it's looking for itself, when it's beyond itself.

Imagine what it takes to master a skill, or pursue a new passion, to try a new hobby, or maintain a lasting relationship.

Remember! The mind is a processor. The brain is stored memory and learned programs.

- When looking for itself; *What am I to be?*

- The mind interrupts itself; *I'll try that over there.*

- When it's beyond itself; *I'm not enough as I am right here.*

The mind interrupts itself, while looking for itself, if what it sees is not enough of itself as it is.

Let's say you're in financial hard times. And you're looking for a secure spot to be. You see someone who is doing well, and you also see *why* they're not in hard times as you are. When you observe them, you believe they're doing well because of what they do for a living. That it makes a secure living even in a bad economy. You think, *I'll do what they're doing. That's what I should do because they're doing fine and I'm not.*

So, out of the blue you make plans. You take classes and get certifications to become what they are. At some point in the process your mind interrupts, *I don't like this. This is so boring. This does nothing for me. I'm not interested in this at all.* The mind interrupts itself while in the process of changing its direction. Why?

Not only is the mind interrupting itself, but it rejects what you're doing. *What is it that is me? What is true to me that will make a living for me?*

THE NUMBER ONE REASON FOR FAILURE

Before the doing of a hard thing is made into an easy thing, the mind will search for a lost self. It's the number one reason for failure in any pursuit. And it is why you must stick close to what's easy for you, before overreaching beyond you.

The journey between what you are now and what you're becoming is perilous. It's fraught with distraction. There are consequences when the processes of the mind filter through the brain's stored memories and unexamined irritations.

As the mind filters through those memories, processing what the brain learns, recall of failure and disappointment will irritate, and say, *I'm not good at this. This isn't my thing. This is too hard.*

You may ask, *What memories and unexamined irritations would cause such thoughts?* Well, it's the thoughts themselves that cause more of the same.

Those opinions, self-criticisms lay dormant until something is difficult. When you struggle to perform an easy way, you're interrupted by past programs. They'll say, *You're stupid. You're crazy. You have no talent. You're worthless.* And though you can't remember where those thoughts came from, if they are triggered while you're learning, what you're learning will be interrupted, because the mind obeys emotions and will filter back through them uncontrollably. At least at first. At least until you can change the filter.

CHANGING THE FILTER

The journey of self-commitment offers prolonged success with new thoughts, new filters. These new filters are simple. They say, *I am good at learning. I am worth the effort.* Now, these are true thoughts. They aren't manipulation, or fake-it-till-you-make-it brain plants. They are honest truths. The other truth is that your return to your learning is dependent upon them.

That's the thing you don't see about those people who are a success in the thing you're looking to become. If you see those who are still doing well, you must consider how long they committed to the same line of work, doing the same thing for a considerable time, through the hard times, which are not evident in your superficial view of their story.

---

if each here is acknowledged,
each where is obvious

ORIENT THE MIND: HERE

What you're doing, whom you are being, how you behave, these are all indicators of where you stand, how solid your footing, and which direction you'll pivot at each turn. Where you pivot effects your destiny. You can either make broad sweeps of misdirection or take small steps, with small corrections. Your choice. And the choice begins with those whispers of an inner voice.

Where you stand right now influences an environment you can't see. That's why you must keep your attention close to the center of each step. Warm the water nearest you rather than trying to warm all the waters of the whole of the ocean. Your job is to proliferate the mind beginning where you are.

- Trust what you're good at.
- Trust what's easy for you.
- Trust what is your nature.

The mystery of self-discovery unfolds within this natural state.

If each *here* is acknowledged, each where is obvious. If you take nothing for granted such as the thoughts that tear you down or build you up, you'll make conscious steps. Focus and begin every day from here. Because it's in that mind that you begin again.

Always, begin again.

Self-Discovery – Chapter 2 – The Mind

1.   **What is the mind that is not your thoughts?**

     a.   curiosity

     b.   notices subtle differences in the environment

     c.   what if?

     d.   what's over there?

     e.   what thoughts are these?

     f.   all of the above and more

2.   **Where does the mind go when you're unaware of where you are?**

     a.   distracted by curiosity

     b.   where you left off

     c.   where you should be

3.   **What does the mind do to scale itself?**

     a.   jumps to new hard things

     b.   runs ahead of you

     c.   begins with what you're good at, what's easy for you

Self-Discovery

Journal Prompt – Get inspired!

Begin with here.

---

the journey of self-commitment
offers prolonged success with new thoughts,
"I'm good at learning. I'm worth the effort."

THE MIND IS TAKEN FROM ITSELF BY TWO, SUBTLE DISTRACTIONS: THOUGHT AND TASK.

When task distracts the mind, it's because something you're doing is easier than the thing you were doing before you got distracted.

But when the mind is distracted by thought, then the thoughts are telling you why you can't accomplish this thing you were doing before you got distracted.

TRY THIS:

Focus on something, just one hard thing you've been unable to get done. And then notice each time you're taken away from it. Notice whether it is a task or a thought.

IF IT'S A THOUGHT:

Examine the thought without attachment to it. Discover the root of the thought, then ask it if it's true. If the thought has no reply, go back to what you were doing. If it does have a reply, then follow where its logic is leading you, because it may solve a problem for you.

IF IT'S A TASK:

If a task has distracted you, then ask yourself what's more important, the thing you were doing or the task itself.

Take conscious notice of how often these distractions happen, and you'll be done with the hard thing you're working on, in half the time it would normally take to finish.

Answers: 1f, 2a, 3c

Journal

Self-Discovery

Journal

Self-Discovery

Journal

CHAPTER THREE

THE SOUL

REFERENCE POINT

We begin this story in a different place than you're used to being every day. Most days, you are focused on a world out in front of you, and everything you see out in front of you is a reference to you. It refers to you. It tells you where you're standing, where you're sitting, what you're doing, and why you're there.

Every reference point that is out in the world, refers only to your body—not your mind, and certainly not your soul.

In this chapter on the soul, we'll be focused on the condition of the soul that *is* the soul. Not what affects the soul, or what is the purpose of the soul, but what *is* the soul.

To tell that story about what the soul is, we first must identify what it is NOT, because what it is not, is just as important as what it is. As you determine what the soul is not, the soul identifies closer and closer to the being you are that is *among* a reference point.

For example, let's say that someone in front of you is annoyed at you. You see on their face their annoyance. That's the only way you know they're annoyed. Or is it?

You probably know they're annoyed because of the way they're breathing, or the way they're standing, or the way they're shouting, even if they're talking about something other than what they're annoyed about. You notice there's some condition of them that isn't really right with them, and therefore, in the way that it isn't right with them, it feels not quite right with you.

Understanding the condition of 'not quite right' isn't in your body. Your body is not picking up those cues, although your eyes are seeing it, your ears are hearing it. You might even be feeling it by the way that they are walking on the floor. But the truth is, the being in you that notices this thing is your soul.

WHAT THE SOUL KNOWS

Your soul knows what feelings are. Your soul knows how to identify feelings. If you are not in touch with that condition of you that is the soul, then *you* get nervous, annoyed, paranoid, and all manner of other feelings, because you don't know that another's annoyance is affecting the condition of your feeling. The soul is telling you, *they're annoyed.*

If you listen to that soul and you understand what that soul is telling you, and you care about whether they're annoyed or not, you might ask your soul, *why are they annoyed?* "They're annoyed because you are standing in their spot," the soul might say.

If the soul tells you exactly what's going on with that other person, it means that you've developed a relationship with the soul.

Your soul cannot see that person. It cannot hear or even feel from your physical body. But what your soul does feel is their soul. Your soul is in a relationship with them in a way that they identify for you through your soul what they're feeling.

People such as autistics, who do not recognize facial features, can identify an emotion someone else is having, without having to identify their facial cues. Autistics tend to look down. They tend to look away. They tend to not engage. But they're engaged. Their soul is engaged in a body that's incapable of fully, neurologically connecting to the facial cues of another person. That neurological relationship is broken. But what's not broken is their soul.

In research studies on autistic children, they have found ways to communicate. The physical expression communication process is damaged. They can't physically express what's going on, what they're thinking, what they're feeling, but they can express when they're not looking, using a finger hovered over a typewriter and just being held in the right spot. Enough organization is going on in the soul that if the right direct communication potential is brought to that autistic child, they will be able to eke out a message.

The soul is not intelligent. It isn't an intelligence. It is an organ, just like the heart, the brain, the kidney, or the liver; it has a function, not an intelligence. So, you can have incredible anxiety and not know where that anxiety is coming from. But if you're tuned in enough, you might find out it's that person right over there in your yoga class who has extreme anxiety affecting you. You've got to be tuned in to that, or you'll be responding to your own anxiety instead of responding to someone else's anxiety, who might need your attention, and your calming reassurance.

THE SOUL IS AN APERTURE

every time the mind looks for *something*,
the aperture to the soul opens up

Think of a camera, an aperture either opens or closes depending on how much light is being brought to the back of the camera, to the digital film. How much light will be in the picture is based on the aperture, or rather the size of the hole in the opening. The soul has an aperture as well. It opens and closes by the mind's curiosity.

When the mind doesn't know what question to ask of itself, for example, to determine what to do, what to be, how to behave, where to go, what to think beyond the thoughts that are programmed in the brain from some event or something someone said, the mind in that instance is looking for *something*.

Every time the mind looks for *something*, the aperture to the soul opens up.

The soul is an organ that provides information, and it's always waiting for you to approach it with information. Let's say you're having a conversation with your father. And your father is always critical of everything you do, no matter what it is, how simple the thing is, if it's an opportunity for him to express his intelligence, he's going to give you information that he either knows, or thinks you don't know that he *doesn't* know. The soul, however, will see right through that.

Your soul knows exactly what he's doing. Why? Because it's in touch with his soul. So, if you can turn off the listening in you that has listened since you were a child, to that part of him that is always so darn critical all the time, if you can turn that off just long enough to hear from his soul where he is, you might hear how afraid he is of not knowing an answer. What does that mean? If he doesn't know an answer? It could be a great anxiety in him. That anxiety is what came into you, and then you became programmed by it. The soul is a foundation of information that can key-in to another human being very quickly, very easily, if you are tuned in to it.

ORIGINS AND THE SOUL

Every soul has its own origin. It originates either from some other dimension, some other world, or right here on Earth. But not every origin is the completion of the soul. So, it may need to move into other dimensions to complete its expansion. In that case, it requires in this lifetime that you become aware of it and aware of its knowledge, which is different than intelligence. It needs *you* to know the way that it knows, before you die, for the soul to expand into the next hereafter.

The soul is what gets left behind when your body passes, and if you aren't really ready for your eternal afterlife, the time that you have spent here on this earth will determine whether your soul reincarnates into your origin or into the last place you were as a being that is physical, or even some dimension between physical and nonphysical.

The foundation of your soul, then, is all about expansion, and it requires the life that you're in to understand the condition of that expansion. It doesn't need to know exactly the foundation of that expansion, like whether you're to be a teacher or a learner, a scientist or an artist, to be somebody's wife or somebody's grandmother—these functions that will play out the expansion of the soul aren't necessarily the condition of a specific.

What is specific is what you learn from being a grandmother, being a teacher, being a learner—these things that are of great importance to specifics about what you learn, determines the level of your awakening and determines the level of that awakening as to whether you've lived it out.

If you haven't lived it out, there is a threat to the soul. The reason we bring this up is that threat is reached *into*. Most threats are external. The threat to your external is reached *at*. For example, an aggressive act is reached at you. A raging tiger running towards you, is reached at you. The fear that comes from that reach creates recoiling, some form of protection, some condition of response. But when it comes to a threat to the soul, it's reached *in*.

Let's say you're close to dying. This is just an example. You're a long way from dying, but as an example, you're close to dying, and you know you're dying, either because you feel it, or the doctors tell you, or you're just old enough to know, *Hey, this is what dying feels like, and I'm dying.* If you span across your life looking for its completion, and your thought is, *I'm not done. I haven't done all I meant to do, everything I wanted to do I couldn't get done in the time that I had,* if that's your thought before you pass, you will not pass in an easy manner. You will fight to complete whatever thought is completed before your body finally releases the spirit.

As your spirit is pulling away from the body, that is a reach in. You're reaching in to know something about yourself, or to lament something about yourself, and that threat to the soul is a threat of life being over. Think about that for a moment.

Think about the idea that the soul never dies, and you're in a thought of, *I didn't complete what I came here to do.* If the soul never dies, and you're thinking, I didn't complete what I came here to do, what does that say to the soul? It tells the soul, *It's over. That's it. That's all you get. That's all there is.* That's a thought within, a threat that is reached in.

The soul, therefore, could very simply decide, *I've got to stay here and finish what I came here to do,* and by doing so, it doesn't follow spirit into the realm of God. It may stay right here with your body as your body passes.

Why do you think that graveyards are haunted? Why do you think houses get haunted? Because there is something in the soul that is bound and determined, determined to stay right here. And it can happen to the most spiritually advanced people on the planet, the most religious people. It can happen to anyone, that they get stuck in the episode of physicality of this life. Because the physicality of this life is a doing, that doing has a physical reference point. It's got people, places, and things that it refers to itself to be. The body trained it that way and told it, *There isn't enough time. I haven't gotten it all done. There's more that I'm to do.* Or there's some level of forgiveness at stake, forgiving one of those reference points, or oneself as a reference point.

CLEANSING EXTERNAL REFERENCE POINTS

To keep the soul cleansed of these reference points, it must constantly be part of something. Whether it's part of you, or part of the way of the earth, or part of the way of the condition of the soul, no matter what it is part of, its function is an organ.

And just like your kidneys or your liver or your heart, the soul's function must keep functioning. The more you do to reference yourself to the soul, the more function it has, and the greater the job it feels it has done, because it doesn't feel like it's supposed to do something to be a part of why it's here, it's just supposed to *be* something—your friend, your partner, your alliance, your reference, the reference point for which you enable communication among others. You help heal the mind of others, the heart of others. You hold that attention fastened among the others as you tune in to your own soul, and your soul tells you what to say, what to feel, who to care about, who to turn away from, because they're no good to you. The soul tells you they just suck off you because they love all your positive attitude, and they want that positive attitude, because they have a terrible, terrible attitude. And they want that positive attitude from you because your soul constantly supplies that for you.

Having a relationship with the soul is very different from having a relationship with God. God is not the initiator of your relationship with God, because God can only give to you what you're willing to receive. If you're unwilling to receive, whether it's positive or negative information, what you're unwilling to receive, God can only benefit you in a place of your admittance, what you admit. But that's not true of the soul.

The soul can be of benefit to you no matter what you receive, no matter what you're willing to admit. If you need to be in denial about something that's too hard to face, because it's just too hard to face right now, the soul can give to you that part of you you're missing in the thing that's too hard to face.

If your thoughts are, *I can't face it because it's too sad, it's too hard, it's meaningless. I can't look at that.* The soul can say to you, "It's okay. You don't need that right now. We're learning how to feel in the face of it all. We're learning what 'feels' in the face of it all. We're learning how to be strong, in the face of it all."

And then you might reply back, *But I've got to face it. I know I have to, because it's right there. And if I don't face it, then I will never be strong enough.* The soul then responds, "We're strong enough. We're always strong enough, we're protected."

But what if, what it shows me is just too sad, what if it's too hard?

"It'll never be too sad. It'll never be too hard."

The soul can say those things because it knows that the only thing that matters is what happens after the body dies. That's all that matters. The soul knows that so long as you face life with your soul, that's all that matters. Because your soul is in the condition of joy, and it will give you joy, even in the face of things that are not joyful, things that are very hard, things that are just downright ugly.

Because the soul is in joy all the time, whether you are or are not, the soul lives in a space of pure joy, and so, that's what it's always looking for or concerned with—your joy.

THE SOUL AND JOY

The soul is always looking for joy. So, when you're sad, it will look for joy, and it may only find joy in chocolate, or it may only find joy in alcohol or marijuana or cocaine. But when it does that, it's only finding joy in the mere moments you're finding joy, the soul responds, "Oh, there it is. I was looking for that. Every time you look over there, I don't see joy and I don't feel joy, and just like you, I'm a little scared of that too. But when you drink or smoke and I feel joy, and we both feel joy, then there we are."

But you've got to know better, because as we said earlier, the soul is not intelligent. It is not an intelligence. It doesn't know what you're doing in your recovery of joy. It just knows *There's joy. I've been looking for it. I've been trying to give it to you, but you wouldn't receive it, so you found it.*

Paradise with the soul is about admittance, however. What do you admit to? "You know that thought doesn't help me at all." The soul tells you that's a bad thought. "We ought not think that thought." The intelligence in you won't tell you that. The greater mind in you cannot reach you. It's the soul that reminds you; because it tells you where joy is. That's a reference point to joy. So, when you finally have a moment away from dark thoughts, the soul is what reminds you what you ought not think.

The soul is not a friend to you the way your guides might be friends to you, or God can be a friend to you. Jesus can be a friend to you. The soul is not a friend to you. The soul is *you*.

The soul is the everlasting you, the you that is forever and cannot die. And because the soul cannot die, it doesn't fear whatever threat you experience from an external reference point.

A friend will tell you to stay away from those things. A friend will tell you, "I don't think we should go over there anymore. I think if we go over there, we could die. It's dangerous." The soul just knows your joy and knows how much joy you feel over there and will want to go over there, over, and over, and over. It will not notice, even in the moment that you die from being over there. So that condition in you that survives, that you might even get stuck over there, because that's where joy was, even though, in the fear your body knew, that over there was bad for you, that fear that held you both in suspension, it has two pulls. It's the pull of joy and the pull of knowing better.

Pull of joy and the pull of knowing better has a certain tension point in it that can trap the soul, if it kills off the body. So, danger from an external reference point is intelligence. Danger from an internal reference point is about being stuck.

Joy is a soul in its true state, but joy *of* the soul can be terminated, when it no longer feels inside you any kind of joy it can hold on to.

The foundation of your joy is in the soul, and the soul must be given that joy, and it's only required in small doses. You don't need big, grandiose things to give the soul joy. Sometimes it's just a hot bubble bath. Sometimes it's just calling up a friend you haven't talked to in a long time. Sometimes it's about cleaning the house, and that feeling of a job well done, because you can see all around you a clean house and you feel good having gotten that done. A soul does not require huge actions, and neither does your life.

---

just being a good person will not satisfy your soul
at the end of your life

Your life does not require you do great things in order to experience the purpose of your life, it only requires that you do things that are in alignment with your awareness of what you can do. Anything you are afraid of that you cannot do, so long as it doesn't take great hurdles over who you are to get it done, then it's absolutely just a matter of pushing forward those 'beings' you are that does.

Being a good person for others is not what we're referring to. Just being a good person will not satisfy your soul at the end of your life. You've got to be good enough at the things you are good at to know they are necessary to someone who is not good at that. You can be a pretty rotten person, meaning somebody who's terrible about making people feel good, and still find your way into heaven.

If what you do that you are good at, and other people are not good at, if it is needed and necessary, you're contributing the part of you that you became, in order to be for someone else who never became that. This is a soul-expanding experience; not how nice you were to animals and other people. It is a waste of a life. Your soul needs more than that. Your soul needs more than you just being nice.

THE EVILS OF NICE

As a matter of fact, just being nice could be stripping you from your very soul's purpose. *Well, I'm a nice person.* You could be so nice that you're too nice to tell people where they belong. *Now, you go over here and you go over here because you're better at that, and you're better at that.* That's a leader. That's not necessarily a nice person. That's someone who's seeing a bigger picture, who acknowledges the good in others and places them where they belong.

Or you might be that person over there who's good at that thing that someone who's a leader told you to go over there to do, and they may not have been very nice about it, and you might have a lot to say about how not nice they are. If you say so to their face, that's okay. But if you say it to all the others who are really nice, it may not be the foundation you need, or your soul needs, to understand the power of that spot of a leader because you need to be smarter than that. The soul will tell you how to be smarter than nice, if you listen to the soul and not all the people you're nice to.

The soul doesn't really care how nice you are. The soul wants to know how well you contribute to those who need to know what you know but they don't know. If say, you're around someone who thinks they know everything, a real know-it-all, and there is nothing you can say that would surprise them in any way, because they'll have something to say about that thing, and they'll come up with something just because they don't want to look like somebody who doesn't know it all or that you had something to teach them, and let's say you feel inadequate because of every response they give to what you tell them.

Do you really think that's *your* feeling of inadequacy you're feeling?

It's probably their inadequacy you're feeling, your soul is telling you, "They feel inadequate. They always feel inadequate.

They always need to tell everybody something, so they feel like they fit-in or have a place. They feel inadequate all the time."

If you hear your soul inform you of another, then you'll know what to say for their benefit: "You know, that's really interesting, and I'm so glad you told me that. I'm really glad you're here, because you know a lot more than I do about these things." That alone makes your soul feel so good. Because your soul feels the good that person feels which you made them feel.

That's not being nice, it's not niceness.

Nice is when you don't make any ripples or waves, and you hold back what you were going to say, for fear that other people won't like you for saying that. That's nice.

When you withdraw and don't be yourself for fear of others' reaction to you. That's being nice.

However, if you say something that somebody else says is dumb, and they may not even use the word dumb, they just walk away because you said it. Then that means you probably said something they needed to know that they didn't want to hear, and if you listen to their feelings, over your own, over your own soul, then you will feel what they're feeling, which is probably something to do with *I feel so stupid. I feel so dumb.'*

---

when you learn how not to be so nice,
your soul gets some air

The response to that, which isn't very nice would simply be, "Oh, I must have irritated you with that. Sorry about that. I'll remember next time not to speak my mind."

SELF-CRITICISM

When you learn how not to be so nice, your soul gets some air. Nice people don't breathe much. They're always holding their breath because they're afraid of what others say. They're always listening for criticism. They don't realize they're listening to their own criticism, and in fact, they're closing off their air because of that criticism. They're listening and listening and listening.

If they were to listen to their soul instead of their own self-criticism, what they would probably hear is, "It's okay, we're okay. Who cares? We're here because we want to be here, you know. And today, let's just rest. Tomorrow, we've got things to do, but today, let's just rest."

But maybe you'll start to feel like the soul doesn't know better, *I rested yesterday, I've done enough resting*, then the soul will go, "So?! Today we rest. What's the deadline?" *Maybe I don't have a deadline. If I just get this part done, then I can rest, then it'll be okay.* That'll be enough for the soul to know that you're thinking about what the soul told you is best for you.

If you do what the soul says is best for you, even if you put the soul aside for a minute, be sure to go back to the soul and say, *I'm sorry I forgot you. I'm back though, I promise. We're resting. We're going to rest.* Then the soul will never feel forgotten.

ONLY BECAUSE YOU HAVE TO

When the soul feels forgotten, everything gets hard, really hard, and nothing can get you up in the morning. Nothing can make you feel like doing anything except what you must do. No one should live a life doing just what they have to do. That's not a life at all.

But let's say that's the kind of life you're living right now. Let's say that every day you get up because you have to; you go to work because you have to; you come home because you have to; you take care of your children because you have to. If everything you do is because you have to, it's because you haven't asked your soul, not even once, what it wants to do.

What if you got up today, and you're getting ready because you have to? What can you say to your soul that would change that attitude? We mean change it so you're *not* getting ready just because you have to. What if you're getting ready because you're preparing for the day?

Let's see what the soul would say to help us get there. *Soul, why do I always feel like I just do things because I have to?* The soul would reply, "Because you forget me all the time. You never ask what I want, you never give me what I want. You never do anything just for me."

The soul will always tell you the truth. It will always tell you what you need. But it won't always tell you what you want. It's not always that smart. *Want* is a condition of the body. The body is always in a state of want. The body wants to fly. It wants to run. It wants to eat. It wants to sleep.

The soul can tell you what you need because it wants to enliven you through your needs.

WHAT THE SOUL NEEDS FOR YOU

The foundation of need is so strong. If you satisfy your need, if you give to your needs, you will build a foundation where you stand that is for all concerned. This is why being nice isn't good, because if you're not satisfying your needs, then you can't satisfy the needs for all concerned.

If you need time to yourself, a nice person won't say, "Look, I need some time to myself." If you need an important sensation such as solitude, great expectations, the feeling of excitement, exploration and adventure, the joy of competition. If you need those things, by golly, your soul will tell you and you must follow.

You cannot just be nice and let everyone run all over you, demanding from you something you just don't have. The reason it's not in you is because you're not giving it to you, therefore the threat is within.

ONCE UPON A TIME - "THE SOLARIUM"

A long time ago, in a land very different from this one, a land with caustic air so bad, people had to wear face masks if they wanted to go outside. The air was filled with toxins. In that land, there were people who looked very similar to how humans look today, with one exception. They had no hair. They had no eyelashes either, nothing on their body, just a slick surface.

The reason they had no hair was because the toxic air had seeped into their food, and that food they ingested, over a long period of time, after two or three generations, eventually wiped out the gene that would produce hair. Now without hair, every time they sweated, the sweat would just roll off, down to the floor, and they would stand in puddles of their own sweat.

Whenever the heat was so hot where they were, such as inside of a solarium, where the sun came in, they would love it, they loved that heat. They relished the heat because it would cleanse their bodies. They would feel cleansed after a good sweat. When all that sweat came pouring out of their bodies, the reason it felt so good afterward was because of what they had ingested in their synthetic world. The toxins were so bad for their bodies that even their sweat was colored a dark gray.

After a while, they didn't even notice the color of their sweat. It just seemed like the color sweat is supposed to be. They had no idea that fresh clean sweat was clear and salty. They just thought it was dark and gray, naturally.

Until one day, someone invented a special booth. It was a tent where they could go in and sip oxygen, pure, clean oxygen. And the people who utilized this great invention called oxygen—fresh, clean oxygen—those people that would utilize the tent, afterward they would go to the solarium for a sweat. And that's when they noticed that their perspiration was clear and clean, like water. They believed it was because they were in a miraculous tent. That the booth was filled with all kinds of special emollients, and all the promises that the sellers made about the tents. They had no idea that it was just because they were breathing clean air that their sweat ran clear.

*****

THE HONEST TRUTH

The moral of this story is that just because the product of your soul shows up on people as a smile, doesn't mean that what's supposed to come from your soul is a smile. There are other things that come from a soul fulfilled. Those things may show up in other people as tears, or rage, or sorrow. But what it is overall is honesty.

What comes from the soul is honest, and the more in touch you are with the soul, the more honest you become. More people will understand you because you're honest, and the more *you* understand you is because you're honest.

In an accelerated self is honesty above all. The harder it is to be in your life, means the harder it will be to be honest. But learning what your soul needs and supplying it for your soul, means the easier it becomes to be honest. Honesty can be delivered in a warm friendly way, but they at least *know* what you're thinking, even if they like what you've said or not.

But remember, honesty does not require an opinion; it requires the truth.

Self-Discovery – Chapter 3 – The Soul

1. **How does honesty reflect on your soul's joy?**

    a. honesty supplies the soul's need

    b. honesty is about listening to what's real

    c. honesty doesn't hide

    d. all of the above

2. **What does the soul enable you to do that you cannot do without it?**

    a. it lets you read people's minds

    b. it can tell you what people are feeling

    c. it lets you dream without sleeping

3. **Why does joy matter to the soul?**

    a. because it survives death

    b. its job is fulfilled by bringing you joy

    c. because it feeds on life

4. **Why does the soul inhabit a body?**

    a. to help others in a way they can't help themselves

    b. to learn from being nice

    c. to expand its existence through a physical experience

    d. to be kind to animals and people

Answers: 1d, 2b, 3b, 4c

Self-Discovery

Journal

Self-Discovery

Journal

CHAPTER FOUR
THE SPIRIT

To know your spirit is to know the part of you that is always filled with hope. Your spirit is never hopeless or down. The spirit is always up.

When your spirits are low, it means the world around you has become stronger than your spirit. But it doesn't really mean your spirit is low. Your head may be hanging low, your mind is in a deep well, or your mood may be low, your soul may even be forlorn, but the spirit cannot be low and still be a spirit.

THE DENSITY OF SOUL, SPIRIT, AND BODY

Of the three aspects of what make up your physical identity, the body is the most dense. The soul is the second less dense in complexity and properties. And the spirit is three times less dense than the soul.

The spirit is the nature of you that is always in its origin, the origin of God. Your spirit is your God Self. When you tune in to your spirit and become of a higher mind, you've entered the God Self.

Sondra is currently in her spirit, or in her God Self, to deliver this message. In fact, she's struggling to stay in it because her physical body is so weak and sick. We may come back to this message when she's feeling better.

But when the body pulls strongly away from the spirit due to illness, the spirit cannot enliven the body. Nor can the spirit enliven the mood, enliven the mind, or the soul. Because the spirit cannot interfere with physical form the way the soul can. The soul can interfere because it has certain conditions of life that need to be met, and those conditions are drawn up from the body. The spirit, however, doesn't need conditions of life to be met; it is eternal and will always live, no matter what the body is going through.

If the body knows how to tune in to the spirit, the spirit might tell the body, *It's okay, you can rest. Rest is what you need. Please rest.* Or the spirit might say, *Let's rally! Let's get something to drink, let's get something to eat, and let's feel better. We'll feel a lot better once we've had a few of our needs satisfied.* The spirit always tells the soul and the body what the condition of life requires.

One day it will tell the body, *Just lay down. Don't get back up. There's no need to get back up—it's time.* When the spirit tells the body that, the body's lived a good amount of time in the conditioning of spirit. Spirit conditions the body to listen to such a message.

When we return, we're going to talk about how the spirit was brought into a physical form, through the nature of the soul into the body, and how to appeal to the body to receive a resurrection from the spirit.

***

Now that we have refreshed, we have slept, and we feel better, we can enjoy this spiritual journey.

Let this remind you that whenever you lose your sense of direction, comfort, or an understanding of where you are, there are things you probably need that you are not paying attention to, that only spirit knows in the way that you need it.

WHAT'S BENEATH YOU CANNOT SERVE YOU

When something is in a dark space, meaning you can't see it, or it's beyond you, or above you, or way below you, it means you're identifying your condition with that thing as relative to you. So, if something is beneath you to do, it means you've set yourself above someone else who would do it.

But when you are destined to serve in some way, whether serving the interest of others, or serving your own interests, or serving a market, serving customers, serving the world, whatever the condition of your serving, whatever opportunity you give to yourself that would otherwise be beneath you, will teach you, and train you the humility you need to serve. Because humility is a practice, and service is a law of that practice.

However, there's a backside of service.

The backside of service is that it depletes your energy. It depletes your sense of self because you give yourself to another, so that the service you provide is something *they* need.

When the spirit needs to rejuvenate you however, when spirit needs to serve you, you need to identify your service is within. This means cutting off all service to things that are outside of you. This doesn't mean turning away from things you think are beneath you.

It's important to identify that part of *you* that needs to serve you: serve your needs, your interests, your spirit, and sometimes that means enlisting the help of others.

Whenever the spirit cannot reach you—you are low in energy, low in conditioning of some kind, you can't see the way forward or beyond, or even just where you are—*you* must call upon the spirit, which then raises up your state of being.

The spirit is in union with the body, such that you could see a resurrection of the body or the soul, through the spirit. Here's how that works.

TO AND AMONG

You may disagree with what we've told you so far as the way to get there, (nothing is beneath you when you serve; humility is your trainer in service), but the only way to get to the needs of the body is to allow the service to occur from the following places: within, above, in, below, to and among.

"To and among" is a concept, not a full-on practice. When you draw spirit to and among, it is a way of structuring your position with spirit. Spirit does not come from outside of you because it's already within, and above the self. However, although you are on the planet, spirit is not. Your feet are, and when your feet are how you position your alignment, it means you're aware of the ground where you stand. But as you position your awareness beyond the body (of the mind, not the position of space) then you're aware of the space within and around you that can be occupied by spirit presence.

To and among are reference points for the spirit. Just as the ground is a reference point for where you stand. The ground, then, *refers* to your feet. To make the space around you a reference for spirit to be among you in your presence, you must identify what the spirit is *to* you. The ground is to you what your feet refer to, so that you stand. If the ground was not a reference to your feet, you couldn't stand, because you wouldn't know where to place them. Your feet would wave in the air and aimlessly flail about.

Now consider the space around you. It is not empty when you refer to your spirit as *among* you.

To and among is a condition of you that is very difficult to describe, but once you understand it and tune in to it, you become more powerful as an individual, as well as very powerful in creation.

ESSENCE OF CREATION

"Creation" is different from creativity or creating. Creation is the state of being that is magical. Creation is magical. It is the condition of enchantment because it is a field or an environment in which your power creates. It's not the creativity, or the essence of creativity that's occurring. It is the essence of life that is occurring from this magical, invisible ooze.

Imagine the essence of life occurring for a moment.

Now, how does the spirit create? It's all around you. Spirit is creating everywhere. Everywhere you look, there is creation. Even among human beings, stuck in a world that is nothing but concrete and glass, there is creation. All that concrete and glass may not have been part of spiritual creation before the birth of man, but it is through the birth of man creation occurred, to build all those buildings of glass and concrete.

forming and formulating—all formation is
conduction of spirit

Let's look at stone as an essence of creation. You might think that stone is simply the confluence of environment mixed with movement; from wind, water, erosion, glaciers, mountains, the fall of mountains, and mudslides. If these are in your mind as to what stone is, then you don't know what stone really is, or even what creation is. Nor do you know how spirit moves. Because spirit isn't just in the wind, the water, the glaciers.

Spirit is also in the gathering.

In fact, it's in the gathering that most of the power occurs within creation. It just happens on a very minute level. The way and reason you cannot see spirit is also the way that creation occurs on such a tiny scale, a scale of forming and formulating—all formation is conduction of spirit.

Spirit is alive. And it is alive in matter when matter lives.

Stone, believe it or not, is full of living matter. There are even some stone structures that have their own being, such as a mountain spirit or a stone creature. The ancients knew this from psychoactive plants that gave them information through journeys and vision quests. The production of glandular cellular processes in collusion with plants create a hyper awareness that modern man refers to as hallucination. But it is not hallucination. It's hyper reality. It is the entrance reality (in trance) where what you see and what you visit enters a spirit plane.

The spirit plane reveals the spirit of all being, of all life, and becomes surreal, or super real in the condition of the experience. That's why these psychoactive plants are called medicine. For the ancient natives of Indian cultures, psychoactive plants are known as big medicine. The small conditions of the human mind can overwhelm the body but the hyper-real view is far grander, a spectacular complex compared to the day-to-day mundane.

---

the lackluster experience of your day-to-day
world is the result of inactive spirit

INACTIVE SPIRIT

The day-to-day mundane can overwhelm the body by its domineering nature. The mundane is overbearing to the body because the body is made up of something grand.

It's made *from* something grand, and it's highly complex. If the body is forced into mundane tasks daily, that are overtly routine or the same day after day after day, unless there is some form of spiritual activity going on behind the scenes, the body begins to lack luster.

The lackluster experience of your day-to-day world becomes the result of inactive spirit.

An inactive spirit usually occurs when the body wears down to such a degree that it can no longer call upon spirit. Meaning, the body only calls upon its fundamentals such as eating and sleeping, and that's all. The body says, *I'm tired.* It says, *I'm hungry. I have munchies.* That's the body's need to satisfy or fulfill something it can't identify, so it's gnawing.

In that gnawing, it wants to chew on something intangible to it, so it will want munchies, sugar, sweet; it craves the sweet of life. If you don't give it the sweet of life, you can produce insulin insecurity in the body.

Which can result in cancers in the organ that produces insulin. This happens when the sweetness is squeezed out of life, when you're always very serious, or life is always so serious.

You need to replace all that responsibility and obligation with fun, joy, and excitement. Spirit has no place in your life if you have no place for joy except through foreign substances that make you briefly forget the mundane. These substances, such as sugar, food, or drugs, work to produce a serotonin effect to occupy the mind that doesn't get enough of it from the things you're doing or being.

WHY SO SERIOUS?

You may be wondering, *How do I draw spirit into my life, so that everything isn't always so serious?* You first need to surrender to your physical needs. You might need to sleep 18 hours a day for three days, to recoup, so that your mind is active in dreams. Making your mind active in the inactivity of the body allows the mind a chance to remember what it is that is not just a drone for your job, to feed your family, or to make your living; there must be something productive going on behind the body's activity.

Spirit is an abundant state. It's in everything that lives. If you are surrounded by what is living, what is life, what is alive, you will find a spiritual connection. Aliveness dwells just below the visible. This is what makes matter live. The life force of a plant is visible under certain conditions. Not only does it express this lifeforce, but it consumes that force. It's a breathing of the essence of life that keeps matter living.

You can tune in to that spiritual nature from a place of pure exhaustion, where you completely surrender to the body, and finally say to the body, *Okay, let's rest. Let's just rest.*

Another way to tune in is to surrender to the body's need for water—pure, clean, abundant water—and gulp down a good pint of it. You will instantly feel a connection that you may not recognize as spirit at first. Tune in to that connection of restfulness or clean water to give to the body what it's seeking, to spring forth life within it. If you tune in to that very subtle nuance after refreshing the body, you can identify what you are that is spirit and come alive in it.

* * *

In the next chapter, we're going to talk more about the body. We'll discuss what the whole construct of what the body is, and where in the body spirit dwells. You'll learn what condition of that body you need, in order to keep spirit in tune, alive, and abundant.

We'll finish today by saying the soul needs the spirit for it to feel alive. When the soul is questioning everything you're doing: where you are, who you're loving, and why, that means you're not tuning in to the spirit. You must tune in to give aliveness to what you're doing, where you are, who you're loving, or how you're being.

If you feel yourself questioning everything, the aperture to the soul opens, and then it's time to get clear answers for spirit to come alive in you.

Self-Discovery – Chapter 4 – The Spirit

1. **What does your spirit need, to come alive in your body?**

    a.   it needs good thoughts
    b.   it needs awareness in the body; via dreams, clean water, being among
    c.   it needs the body to exhaust itself with exercise

2. **How does the body generate the feeling of 'the spirit is among'?**

    a.   by imagining the space around the body is filled with spirit
    b.   by setting one's mind 'to and among' as one reference point for the body
    c.   by sensing the presence of spirit
    d.   both a and b
    e.   none of the above

3. **Why does the everyday mundane create a lackluster experience in the body?**

    a. because the spirit is in another dimension from the body and must connect to it away from demands of everyday routine

    b. because the mind is overstimulated by tasks with deadlines, offering no life for the spirit

    c. because the spirit is alive through dreams and vibrancy, it requires the magic of creation, or the body is only an automaton for work and family demands

    d. none of the above

    e. all of the above

4. **What is the aspect of you that is your God Self?**

    a. your soul

    b. your mind

    c. your spirit

    d. your heart

Journal Prompt – Get inspired!

Christians have a way of saying one is 'filled with the holy spirit.' And in that way, they describe a phenomenon that captures the sense we've called, 'to and among.' The experience of that sensation is why people like to gather in holy places such as synagogues, churches, and temples.

They attend services because they feel a raised spiritual essence, in these gatherings with their faithful brethren.

The experience offers a lift, a holy lightness that is difficult to describe but also not easy to recreate in everyday life. So, to experience it, you must create it in yourself, otherwise you only experience it at church.

Some people feel a raised sensation of spirit at Christmas time, or other holy holidays. There's a spirit about the world that shifts the mundane, to a special magical substance that permeates the atmosphere. For some, they experience it when reading sacred texts. Others feel it when they volunteer in groups to help the poor and the dying, or when they help animals find a home. Have you ever felt it? And if so, when has it occurred?

Write about your experience. Write about that sense of a raised spiritual essence. Try to express how it feels in your body. What do you witness in the body? Try to recreate it in yourself, alone.

Answers: 1b, 2d, 3e, 4c

Self-Discovery

Journal

Journal

CHAPTER FIVE

THE BODY

Welcome to the body.

There isn't much the body does on its own in the way the self accelerates, meaning it's the actions *upon* the body that determine acceleration.

Now, we have yet to exactly define what acceleration of the self really means, but it's in this section about the body where the accelerated self starts to show up. It shows up in ways of joy, giddiness, laughter, and sometimes sorrow, feeling sorry for those who don't understand the condition of your acceleration. This is because to accelerate means moving beyond emotional base conditions in the body, and into the fantastic condition.

THE FANTASTIC – INVIGORATED INDUCTION

Let's look at the word fantastic for a moment. It's difficult to understand what we mean about this condition of fantastic in the way you feel, in the way you exert yourself, in the way that you experience others, and in the way that others experience you. The fantastic condition is related to fanship. If someone is your fan, then they have a fantastic relationship with you. If you are someone's fan, then you have a fantastic relationship with them. If you are a fan of God in your life, then there is a fantastic relationship with God. The condition of fantastic in the body, as it relates to the accelerated self, is one of *invigorated induction*.

INDUCTION IS WHAT'S BROUGHT "ON TO"

Induction in the body is when something is brought *on to* the body—it's not brought *from* the body or brought *to* the body. It is brought *on to* the body.

For example, you can have an induction of joy, or an induction of sorrow, an induction of excitement, or forlornness. These conditions are not brought *to* you but brought *on to* you. They are an *informed* state; in form—*in the form*—*of the form*, and they are induced in the form. Joy is not brought to the body, it's induced in the body. And then joy becomes a generation, it generates in the condition of its induction.

USE SUPPLY INDUCTION

You can see what we mean with exercise. When you exercise, you have an immediate uplift of energy, as if the body that is given *to* exercise is given exercise. You give to the body exercise and the body responds in a giving. When it's given energy, it's been given a fulfillment of life. It's a fulfillment of life because an accelerated heart rate means an acceleration of oxygen, and in that acceleration of oxygen, there is a *use supply*. What is used is also supplying, therefore exercise is a use supply. The more you use the body, the more it supplies the body.

And then there are diminishing returns if you exercise a lot, and your body starts to wear down, then it needs time to recoup. In its recuperation, it builds stamina in that exercise. The more exercise you can do, the longer your stamina for exercise becomes.

We are talking about induction. Because what is in the accelerated self is an induction supply, which is not the same as what's brought to the body. What's brought to the body, the body responds to. What's induced by the body, the body is giving to. So, when the body is induced into a bad mood, it's usually because someone induced a mood by something that was said, something that was done, or something that reverberated off the atmosphere in a room. The body was *induced* into another experience.

Since this can occur in the way of an effect, it can also have an opposite ability, which means to effect *it*. You can induce your own experience. Let's say you're brought into a room where people are in a bad mood or they've just heard something very souring, let's say at work, and suddenly the morale is dropped because layoffs are starting to happen. And then you walk into that room where everyone else has been filled-in but you, and you see their faces, you feel the energy, the tension, the anxiety, the fear.

You can either be induced by that atmosphere or you can induce a new atmosphere. We don't recommend you enter a room where everybody's just been told, *Some people are going to get fired!* and then say, *Hey! This could be good news for you, for me, this could be a new opportunity if I happen to be the one on the chopping block!* We don't recommend you attempt to induce a mood change in everyone else before you first induce the right mood change in you.

INDUCTION IMMUNITY

Once you build up an immunity through this induction, you're immune to the effect of others on you. Then, in that immunity, you can create that effect on others. It may be an hour later; it may be something you can't even hold onto an hour later. It's just something you know you must do to survive the potentially devastating moment. You're inducing a change in the body so that the body is immune to what has been brought to the body or attempted to induce within the body.

Now, the body, like other aspects of the self that we've discussed—the soul, the spirit, wounds so forth, the mind especially—these are highly complex topics difficult to encapsulate. We're only giving you portions of these topics. When all these topics are brought together in the end of this book, you'll see how they interrelate in a way that builds you into a higher state of your being, rather than suppresses your state of being. This is because you're only functioning in 20% of your being, based on your experience in the world and how the world is attempting to create itself.

As the world attempts to create itself, you either must create yourself in the process of that world, or you fall through the cracks of that world, unless you identify the condition of you that is separate from the world. And believe it or not, even though it seems as if your body is among the rest of the world, it is very separate from the world and yet tied completely with your soul, your spirit, your mind, and your wounds.

The body is an environment of its own. That environment is built on what it breathes, what it eats, how it sleeps, where it sleeps, what kind of interactions it has or doesn't have, but the thing that the body is most intertwined with, above all others—let's see what you think it is! Just think for a moment. What is your guess? Is it mind? Is it soul? Is it spirit? Is it wounds? Which one of these conditions of the self is the body most intertwined with, if it is separate from the world?

INTERTWINED WITH THE BODY

It's the soul. This is because the soul is around the body or among the body. It is *among* it. If the body is in a state of trauma, the soul can flee from the body or what psychologists call "dissociate" from the experience itself. You're looking down at yourself experiencing the trauma.

Often the people with long stares, that thousand-mile stare, have these little blank spots because their body has experienced some sort of psychological or physical trauma. In the dissociative state, the soul doesn't separate from the body. It can't fully leave the body behind, (although it's not impossible), but the soul lives somewhere beyond the body, leaving the body to function on its own.

When the body is functioning on its own, without an interaction with its own soul, there's a vacuousness, a vacancy that goes on in a person's eyes that you can usually detect. You don't see emotion, you see lack of emotion. You don't see investment, you see lack of investment. And these people aren't aloof as they are usually pretty rote, and functioning as best they can without their soul engaged in the body. Sometimes you look in their eyes and see a shadow, not because there's something dark about them but because they've experienced their own darkness. This darkness within comes from loneliness, fear, terror, or nightmares, and the soul is hovering somewhere *about* the body, instead of engaged *in* the body.

Now, just because you or someone you know has experienced trauma, or even just electrified moments of frightening drama in childhood doesn't mean they're soulless. It just means their soul needs to re-enter the body fully, to re-engage in the enlightened feeling of the body.

These are often people who, if they don't get exercise or if they don't get physical fulfillment of some kind, they suffer.

In men, this often plays out in over-sexualized behavior or fantasies. This is because it's an activity where there is control, but in reality it's depression, where the physical body gets a short-lived experience of excitement. And that's all this individual knows as a way to go beyond a feeling of soul dissociation; its disconnection from the body.

In women, the process is often depression with poor eating habits or other forms of addiction. Depression can be its own addiction as well, even if it doesn't result in some sort of habituation. Women can also have sexual addictions in the same way as men, for short-lived experiences of fulfillment, elation, or excitement.

But the body is capable of so much more induction than just simply trying to induce excitement. The body can experience an induction of energy, and it can generate its own energy. That's why exercise can be so addictive for some people because it generates the condition where the body experiences its own acceleration.

LIBERATION TO THE BODY

When the soul experiences the body's acceleration, the soul starts to yearn for the thing being accelerated in the body. Sometimes that's joy of competition or joy of liberation, finally being liberated from that thing that has held them back, whether it's doubt, an ex-boyfriend, or an overbearing, short-tempered parent. When that thing is finally gone, the liberation of that thing brings about a whole new life fulfilled in the body.

The body is drawing the soul back into that experience of life in liberation. The soul and the body are so intertwined, that when the body suffers the soul suffers, too. Conversely, when the soul is satisfied, the body also feels satisfied.

DISEASE

But since the soul is intertwined with the body and the processes of the body, it inhabits the body's weaknesses. We're talking about processes related to genetics, to evolution, or to cultural influence from family line here—not the individual.

This includes everything from skin color to hair color, to ways certain diseases and conditions of the body come about. These conditions are related to the health and well-being of the genetics or the culture that passed down weaknesses or strengths, which interact in the environment. "Diseases" may come about from this interaction, and we use quotes because any disease that occurs in a body is due to a weakness *brought to* the body, whether emotional, psychosomatic, psychological, spiritual, the evolution of the soul, or the evolution of the environment or the body. Diseases are based on weaknesses in the characteristics of the body, not in the individual.

Disease does not come about through the weakness of an individual or their character. It can, but it's rare. It's rare that one's character will cause a disease. What happens instead, however, is that personality can be influenced by disease already in the processes of the body, as the soul orients itself in the body.

This is important to know in the accelerated self because you can have the highest acceleration of your nature, in the joyous joy of your holy way, and still succumb to disease. Disease is a process of breaking down the body. It's not always a process of the condition of the body. It's about breaking it down. If disease is about breaking down the body and, as we said, emotions have a way of disrupting the body, then what does that mean for how the body breaks down because of emotion?

I'm sure you've spent the day in bed because your emotions were off. Some people spend an exorbitant amount of time in bed because they never get the right emotion to click on. So how is it then, if disease is a breaking down of the body, and as we said, character is never the determiner of disease, then how is it that the body can break down or be down and unable to rally when emotions or certain character is not managed? Or at least managed in a way that the body is given a state of acceleration?

This is what happens.

Thoughts are a condition of the body, not the mind. Although the mind is a condition of process, and it processes thoughts, it is the brain, which is a function of the body, that is generating a physiological effect from thought, which is bringing the body down; breaking the body down. The brain and the thoughts the brain keeps diminish energy, diminish mood, and diminish the conditions of the body that would give you a sense of an accelerated self, which would put you on the track to excellence. That's what accelerated really means. It means on the track of excellence.

EXCELLENCE

Excellence is the condition of the body that seeks the best of itself, that wants the most for itself. When the body's on that track of excellence, that means the mind is calling from a state of accelerant. The accelerant is coming from thought, or rather the mind that is invested in the spirit, which is induced into the soul's interaction through the body.

The soul is seeking itself within the activity of the body. In its seeking of itself within the activity of the body, the body becomes enlivened by what it can do, what it knows, and how it performs. When the body gets feedback from what it's really good at, its activity is being generated by new thoughts, new ideas, new ways of thinking about itself: *Well, what if? You know, maybe I'm not good at that. But I know what I am really good at!*

WHAT YOU'RE GOOD AT

When you focus on what you're really good at, you get a charge in the body. You're getting feedback. It feeds back to you that you are good at that, either from other people's compliment or from your own compliment, your own observation.

Maybe you're an amazing mathematician, and for fun, you like to do math puzzles. And in the result of doing those math puzzles, you find out how good you really are because you solve them, one after the other, after the other, after the other. And people may think that this is the process of your mind that is interpreting these puzzles and solving these puzzles, but it is a function of the body interacting with the mind.

Have you ever watched someone solve a puzzle? What is their body movement? What is their behavior? How are they sitting? How are they holding their face? How are they holding their eyes? How are they squinching their mouth, holding their pencil?

When they're solving a problem, it is the body that is resolving that problem, because it is the reference point of the body. As we discussed before, what is your reference point? In a problem, it is the reference point of the body that is interpreting the condition of the problem which is to be solved. Therefore, when it is solved, the body is accelerated with excitement! Enthusiasm! A thrill! It is a physiological induction of self—what I *can* do!

Let's imagine a robot. Imagine a robot getting excited about what it can do. That doesn't happen, does it? Robots are programmed to do what they do by the programmer. The programmer is solving a problem and using a robot to complete the solving of that problem, and the robot has no emotional response whatsoever to its ability. Why?

You might say it's because robots don't have emotions, they're just circuits and wires and processes of electronic computation. Is your brain not also that? You may not have hardware, you have wetware, but it's essentially the same thing, biochemical processes that are identifying a condition of a problem to solve and solves the problem.

the more you learn what you are through the
process of what you can do,
the more your body comes alive in who you are

So why is a physiological process in a body different from a robotic process? It's another function of the body already built-in to your character. It is the joy of self.

The joy of self, *What can I do? What have I learned that I already know how to do?* It's also a joy of learning, *What am I? What. Am. I? I am. What am…? I am learning. I am brilliant. I am beautiful. I am extraordinary. I am learning.*

These are the conditions of *I Am* that is the self, a grand accelerated self, a self that is learning what it is. And the more you learn what you are through the process of what you can do, the more your body comes alive in who you are, what you are, and why you're here.

EXPRESSED FROM MULTI-DIMENSIONS

The goal in understanding why the body is a condition of the self—not just a robot with no emotion, no feeling—is that the condition of the body is induced of the self. It is an induction of the self because you are here in a three-dimensional construct that is expressing itself from a multi-dimensional state of being.

Every moment, if you pay attention, you experience who you are in reflection and feedback from what you do, what you think, and what you retain of what you learn. And every condition of that nature of self is a reminder of what condition of you is to be here; *why* you're here.

In the next chapter, we're going into deeper versions of the mind, how the mind and the body, the soul and the spirit, all intertwine to process through your foundations, and in that foundation, what you learn in the grand design.

Self-Discovery

Self-Discovery – Chapter 5 – The Body

1. **What is induction that the body responds to?**

    a. it is the mind that that the body responds to

    b. emotion is the induction that the body responds to

    c. the self is induction that the body responds to

2. **Why is emotion an induction by which the body responds?**

    a. because emotions are a use supply

    b. emotion is induction to the body because you can directly affect emotion

    c. because the body can be diminished by emotion

    d. answers b and c

3. **What is the body to the soul?**

    a. the body is the soul's vessel

    b. the body is the way the soul experiences the 3-dimensional construct

    c. the body is the soul's identity

    d. answers a and c

4. **Where is the soul to the body?**

    a. the soul is among the body

    b. the soul hovers above the body

    c. the soul is in the heart

    d. the soul is in the mind

5.   **Where does the soul influence the body?**

    a.   through emotions

    b.   through disease

    c.   through joy

    d.   through its connection to the body

6.   **Why is the body's sense of what it can do an experience of joy?**

    a.   because of the ego

    b.   because the soul's identity is reflected in what it can do

    c.   because the form reflects what it is through what it can do

    d.   none of the above

Journal Prompt – Get inspired!

INDUCTION:

Put yourself in those moments just before you see the people who make you nervous, anxious, or annoyed. Inspired by the excerpt below, from the chapter, how do you induce a mood that alters your approach to being with them? How can you use the induction phenomena to your advantage when working with people you don't like?

---

once you build up an immunity
through this induction,
you're immune to the effect of others on you

Answers: 1b, 2d, 3d, 4a, 5c, 6c

Self-Discovery

Journal

Self-Discovery

Journal

CHAPTER SIX

TRUE VERSUS UNTRUE

Today's lesson is going to expose true, once and for all. But first, we begin with its tricky counterpart.

THE UNTRUE

When you're in the spirit of getting things done, there's a mental condition where you know exactly what you need to get done. But there are times when you don't know what to get done. And times you don't know where you're going or even how to begin. Maybe you know the problem you're trying to solve, but maybe the problem isn't clear enough to solve. It's in these times you have to find a way to interact with your mind when there's no awareness of how to complete a task.

These are conditions of untrue.

Untrue is a disconnect from what's true because the true has yet to culminate. It has yet to appear as something you fully understand and can connect yourself with.

The condition of untrue is the state of not being able to connect yourself; when you're disconnected from yourself, you're disconnected from outcomes.

What's the cause of disconnection from an outcome? It's this simple mental structure: *I don't know what the outcome will be, and any condition that is the outcome is untrue to me, because it's disconnected from me.*

GUIDANCE SYSTEM

True, in the way we mean true, is a word that's all about a guidance system—true north on a compass for example. Or a perfectly honed arrow. This arrow has a guidance because there are no curvatures or faults, the shaft is straight and true. The arrow is free of faults that are untrue to the direction you fling the arrow. A flawless condition of the shaft is what makes its guidance true; true to the aim and true to the target.

When the aim is true, then the guidance or the direction of that arrow is true to how it is honed. To hone an arrow requires a great deal of observation. But that observation is not just in the outcome, it's in how it is shaped at each stage. The choice of the wood, the way it's cut from the source, and the way its honed. It's the condition of shaping that determines whether the arrow will be true or untrue. Or whether you can predict its direction and how it will behave through the air, or space between the bow and the target.

When it comes to your spirit's interactions with the world, which is how you relate spiritually to your world, the true is based on a guidance system within your interior. The interior guidance system must be built on some kind of true. Here's how to imagine that.

If your guidance is utilized through a compass, your compass must be true to north. If it is not true to north, if it is untrue to north then whatever direction you head in will be off, or askew, by the percentage that your true is off or untrue. Your interior guidance must align to true, for that reason alone.

UNTRUE LOVE HURTS

Let's say you guide yourself to love in your life. And you guide yourself to love based on feeling, how you feel about someone. But let's say the feeling that feels like love to you is associated with an untrue guidance. Maybe love is associated with a family member you can't get the right attention from, or any attention at all, or maybe the attention you do get is based on criticism or something that you always have to change or adjust for them. Then, that untrue feeling that love is associated with is about falling in love with an askew state of love. It means your true is not honed to the higher self.

The higher self will recognize the difference between what is true and what is untrue because the higher self is askew only to spirit.

THE OUTCOME

When *spirit* takes you askew, it's because your guidance or your direction needs to be moved away from whatever you're focused on. As a result of spirit guiding you, you may feel disconnected to an outcome of where your head is on a subject.

So, true versus untrue, when you learn how to create a guidance system within, and you align that guidance system with what you're doing on the outside, then you will always be connected to spirit, not necessarily to an outcome.

Let's look at what that creates in your view; what it creates in the world you see around you.

THE REGISTRATION POINT

Your being is in your heart, at the center of the crosshairs of internal guidance. The mastery lines extend from the heart out through the head and above it, down to the feet and below them. Then the left to right line intersects at your heart to stretch just beyond each of the shoulders. Finally, another line extends from the heart stretching through your being as the in and the out.

The cross points are moving in to out, left to right, and up to down. This is the kind of crosshair awareness that can orient your internal guidance through registration with Spirit. When the inner compass is tilted to a specific axis, tuning to the right frequency, you'll know when something is untrue because of how that thing tilts away from the guidance within.

Maybe you're asking, *But how do I build that? How do I build a registration point so that when I am in a situation which requires certain guidance, I'm guided with it. How does that become a universal identity within me?*

The answer is not so easy to describe although the process is simple.

IDENTIFICATION AND DELINEATION

Two things allow for internal guidance, and they are rarely ever considered. These things are identification and delineation. Identification (ID) is the I am. Delineation is what follows the I am. *I am hungry, I am stupid, I am strong, I am sorry, I am elected, I am loving.* These I ams are the process of delineating the condition of what you are.

The definition of delineate is to describe or portray something precisely. But if you delineate based on some parental description of what you are for example, then you are not aligned to the correct ID. The ID is inaccurate when it's programed by some self-reflection originating from outside of you, or from your past.

A common example of this false delineation is how a parent may perceive you. Their view will be filled with all kinds of filtration of self. Such as the way they see themselves in you, the way they see themselves *not* in you, and even the way they understand the condition of being a child, because they were once a child, too. Your I ams can be filled-in by all kinds of words of delineation that they have induced in you, until you reprogram to delineate based on the interior guidance system instead. This guidance is that you are a child of God or a child of the source of infinite being.

Because as a child of the source of infinite being, you are not your parents' child. The habits and the descriptions of being that are in a mother and in a father are only relevant up and until you identify yourself (I am…) from a place of being, as opposed to a place of structure.

BEING VS. STRUCTURE

I am tired is not a place of being, it's a place of structure. The structure is what gets tired. Being cannot be tired. Being never gets tired because it exists. Being is always being.

If how you are being however, is in the appearance of tired, it's because your body is in the physical manifestation of wearing down. Maybe the body needs energy, maybe it needs food, maybe it needs rest. The conditions of being on the other hand, are based on what is primitive or primal—not what is associative.

BEING AS ASSOCIATIVE

Associative means, let's say, you're in the company of someone you love, and you enjoy their company. The being, or associative being, is based on their company, which might be feeling romantic. *I am romantic, I am affectionate, I am loving.* These are the beings based on an association with another. But you can be those things without association.

You can be loving without someone in your presence. You can be romantic without someone you are romantic toward. For example, you can be romantic in life or have a romantic relationship with nature, or the universe, or better yet, with God. You might think those are associations. But they're not and here's why.

PRIMARY VS. ASSOCIATIVE

The reason a romance with God is not associative but primary, is that in many ways God is an illusion, because you can't see God. You might be able to hear the voice of God in your head, but even that is a delineation of what 'I am.' *I am in God hearing* is not an association because God is not an entity. God is being within your being, *within I am being*. You are also in the being that is true. Therefore it's primary. It's one. In this one you are being, is a direct connection with the guidance—this is the guidance condition: *I am guided. In God's being, I am guided.* Another primal guidance is worth your daily practicing.

I AM LOVING

I am loving is a state of being that is primary and not associative. *I am loving* is the primal condition *within me* that is loving.

If you practice that condition, *I am loving*, you create primal guidance; your true north, which means *I am love,* but it's is in the active sense.

As a verb, loving manages the mind appropriately. It doesn't even have to be toward the self or toward another. It is a being of its own. If a statement in the mind is a being of its own and can exist within itself, unassociated with anything or anyone else, it is true, it is primary, it is one. It is a true identification delineation. *I am* is the ID, *loving* is the delineation that is true. Here's what we mean.

The brain doesn't quite grasp *I am love*, because it doesn't understand what the vastness of that statement means. But to say *I am loving* is to create a practice of an action you are taking. And the action you are taking is primary, or primal. *I am loving* is therefore what creates your guidance system.

When your guidance system in the true begins with something as definitive and as identifying as *I am loving*, you're getting to the core of your own being. At its core is the in, out, up, down, left, and right. Because you are a sphere. You can create a sphere of awareness and clarify the whole state of you, in the being of you. That is the registration mark to identify what is true.

Now that we've defined the core essence of what is true and untrue, and how you build the guidance system to determine true and untrue, when you build that guidance system, you're more aware of how people, places, and things that either feel or don't feel right, as it is based on *I am loving* as your primary guidance. It is the core of what is true from your guidance of true. But the next question is, *What is the basis of delineation for the I am?*

THE PRIMARY CAUSE IN DELINEATION

When you follow *I am loving* as your guidance, *I am loving* is the cause. Relative to the cause is *be*cause.

Here's what we mean.

The question of delineation is always "What is the cause?" When *I am loving* is the cause, it's the primal state of being. This state is the cause within you, it's the cause of you, and the cause is for you. *I am loving.*

But if you are feeling another system: *I am anxious, I am uncomfortable, I am unsure, I am unaware,* these are establishing where you are that is of the loving *NOT*, or of the true not. So, if you know where you are, (true north), relative to what is making you uncomfortable, you can guide into what is true, and it helps you solve the question of your direction. Here's how.

In the uncomfortable state of being, learn how to ask yourself: *What is making me uncomfortable? Is it physical or something else? I am physically uncomfortable because it is hot. I am emotionally uncomfortable because there is tension in the room. I am spiritually uncomfortable because these people around me know nothing of spirit, and they are encased in some form of darkness that I don't understand.*

Every one of these uncomfortable *be*causes can make you hot, ill-at-ease, out of yourself, so it's critical to precisely identify the cause or the condition.

THE CONDITION

The untrue condition is outside of you. The true condition stays within you. Being focused internally: in, out, up, down, left to right, and delineating *I am loving* as your true north, the compass, establishes the askew or untrue cause. When the compass is being skewed away from the true, then you more easily identify what is untrue to you or disconnected from you.

You may have to get very specific about why you are uncomfortable. *I am uncomfortable because this person who is talking to me is being unreal, insincere. I am unaware of their intentions because they are hiding their intention.*

I am loving as true north can also correct your discomforts. Our neighbor has a son with a disability, maybe it's Tourette's. He'll walk up and down the street and shout to himself. You can't always hear what he's saying. He mumbles to himself and he talks to himself as he walks. This could make someone very uncomfortable if the *I am loving* is not engaged as a guidance, because it feels uneasy to deal with something you cannot understand or are unaware of. The guidance *I am loving,* opens your capacity to be compassionate for what makes you otherwise uncomfortable.

UNTRUE LOVE

Let's look at love. How do you know when love is true love or untrue? The truth is that every individual is dealing with some form of filtration in their association with another. Unless they know where to find what is their own guidance system in the true, it's very difficult for you to determine whether the love that you are sharing with another is true or untrue. And it's difficult for them to identify within themselves what is true and what is untrue.

Therefore, in situations where you are very insecure, it can feel like an untrue love because they don't know how to deal, either with their insecurities or yours. They are unaware of what about you they're supposed to be responding to, so they may respond wrongly. This is because you've chosen someone to love based on what you determined love to be as you were growing up. And the true versus untrue is based on some preliminary conditions of what love was associated with, and many of those conditions of what love is, is untrue to love.

THE PARENT EFFECT

I know this is hard to believe, but your parents have no idea how they raised you. They raised you by the seat of their pants. There was no instruction manual in what to do when you remind them of all the things about themselves they are uncomfortable with.

When they reach those uncomfortable places—*I am uncomfortable, I am unaware, I am unable, I am insufficient, I am insecure*—when they delineate the ID from that place, they put that ID as a mirror to you, so that you feel *I am insecure, I am unable, I don't know how to be who I am, I don't know who I am*. This is because the being that you are as a child of your parents, the delineation of the ID is a blank line.

I am will delineate to a blank line until it's filled in. Therefore, *What am I?* can complete itself in some insufficiency, *I am stupid*.

The blank line in your childhood is an incredible power structure that when wrongly identified by your parents or siblings, it can warp and tug until your insecurities alter your own information about yourself; what you're good at, what you're made of, and what's unique to you gets buried by someone else's ID of you.

THE STAR ABOVE YOUR HEAD

[Note from Sondra: In the original recording of this content, our neighbor we mentioned earlier, is shouting, "Tell the Christmas story! Tell the Christmas story!" We had to honor it.]

True north is a Christmas story. Let's look at something that is in every predominant religion—it's known as the Christmas star. If you look at the Hindu Om, there's a diamond on top, then there is a crescent shape below it. If you look at the symbol for Islam, it also has a crystalline feature, there's a star and a crescent. If you look at the Star of David, that is a crystalline feature, like the star of Bethlehem, or the Christmas star.

If you make that star your true north, then you will find an explosion of awareness. Imagine that star above your head. It is within the mind and above it. It's power is in its brilliance shining upon you and through you. All the enlightened historical figures, in the ancient iconography, have a halo effect that glows all around them. The halo is illumination from an enlightened state, which comes from what is known as the Christmas star, or the Star of Bethlehem, the Star of David.

I call this condition the Christ.

You might say, *But wasn't Jesus the Christ?* Jesus was enlightened by the star. The Star of Bethlehem pointed to his birthplace. Symbolizing that he was born under the star, a child of the Christ, a Christ child. The meaning of what Jesus was in this phenomenon has been lost to time and translation.

But in this universal star, the symbol of illumination comes from the Great Being, the great void from within. This star illuminates the void. You can also see that in the Hindu Om, the void is represented by the crescent or bowl under the diamond. And what came out of the void was the Brahma, or the condition of creation. Life came out of that.

THE TRUE CAUSE

You can test whether that is true or untrue if you tune in from your interior to find the Christmas star, and hold it. All that is true based on the condition *I am loving* will show you the love in all and give you a reason to be the love in all. In that being that is love in all, awareness comes to you.

AWARENESS OF BECAUSE

Why am I so uncomfortable? From a love-in-all perspective, *I am uncomfortable because the person that I'm working with, that I am with, is somehow not loving, needs loving. To protect my own loving, I will go into my contained state of loving. I will find the true. I will be the true; the true that is the true aim of the guidance within me.*

LIBERATION

All guidance must begin in the true for it to be true. If you try to guide from the untrue, you will find incompletion, incapacity, intuitive blocks, fog, resistance, conflict, and liberation.

When you liberate, it's because you don't know what you are that deliberates. Deliberation is to weigh the costs, to weigh the condition. Deliberation is long and careful consideration. Careful consideration means to find the aim that is true. When you are liberated from the aim that is true however, you are detached from it.

Liberation by definition is the act of setting someone free from imprisonment.

[Sondra asks] *So God, how can the untrue liberate you?* Well, here's the crux of the reason why this is part of this program, what true and untrue is and means, and why it's so significant when it comes to the accelerated self.

When you align to the true, it's not an imprisonment the way you think of prison. It is imprisonment in true. To align to the true you cannot waver into the untrue without a great deal of problem, trauma, and malfunction.

TRUE IS BOUND

True doesn't mean you are bound, but it *does* mean you are bound. Guidance in the true doesn't mean you are restricted, but it *does* mean you are restricted. The true guidance doesn't allow you to lie, to cheat, to misdirect. You can't even be depressed or sad for very long, because sadness and depression are states of untrue. The state of untrue can absolutely mangle and warp your guidance system, if you are attempting to make good on who you are, and why you were born and in the world, why in the world, *What in the world am I supposed to do with my being?*

As long as you are in the true, your being is guided by what's true. And it doesn't always mean that you have to align to a configuration you don't understand. *I don't know what the truth is! I can't find the truth! Nothing about this feels right. Nothing about this is right!* Well, the only thing that is true, then, is you! You are the core of that. Keep in the core of that. And what is true appears, it naturally starts to appear. Stay in the true and all that is untrue will eventually disappear, because your guidance is a very narrow path. That narrow path sustains you, keeps you on course, on path.

And there are days where you are working in the blind, days where it is so blind it seems like you'll never be aware of why you're here. But I promise you, the reason that you're here is an outcome you belong to. Therefore, all the true that you are and remain becomes the true that is you forever.

THE REAL YOU AND YOUR POTENTIAL

In review, the accelerated self is a guided system. What is it guided by? It is guided by *I am [delineation]*, and if your delineation is true, the accelerated self excels to a point of great potential. It's always great potential.

Every potential becomes a new actual. Every new actual becomes a foundation. Every new foundation is a platform from which you are to spring. The accelerated self can move swiftly forward only when it is in the true.

The accelerated self moves in an unstable manner when it is untrue. And you can be working toward the true in the middle of a whole lot of untrue that you have to unpack and discard in order to find you are true.

WHAT'S REAL

One last thing, true is the embodiment of real. The more real you are, the more true you are. The more true you are, the more real you are. This doesn't mean that you always tell people exactly what is true. It means you are in the state of being the true; and everything you say comes thereafter as an expression of truth.

We hope that this chapter gives you a whole lot of questions in your mind to get closer to what is true.

The following story demonstrates the difference.

THE BICYCLE

There was once a little boy who had all he could want, whenever he asked for it. Then, one day, a little girl came along on a sparkly new bike.

Now this bike wasn't that fancy, at least not in the way of fancy from a store. But this bike had things upon it. It had things below it. It had things and things and things. This little girl had completely decorated her bike without a square inch undecorated so that when she rode it up and down the street, it made sounds, and it glistened in the sun.

It was so fantastic that when she rode past you in the street, her taillights winked at you as if the very bike knew you were admiring it.

This bike was so beguiling it would enchant every girl and boy she rode by.

Now this little boy who always had the pick of his want, he saw this bike, and the spectacle it made. He ran to his mom to obtain it. "Mommy, mommy, please!" He pleaded. "I must have it!" He stomped. "Please! It must be mine," he whined.

But when his mother actually saw what he wanted, her heart sank. Because she knew no amount of money would be enough. So, she turns and begs her little boy to find something else because there's no way that little girl would give him such a brilliant thing. There was no way that this bike, made so specially for the girl, could be recreated or delivered to anyone but to herself.

But the boy persisted because he was used to getting what he wanted. The little boy believed that what he wanted was what he *needed*, and therefore his crying and pleading, protesting, and tantrums became impossible for his mother to withstand.

She hoped to placate his sobbing and screaming by going to the little girl's mother and offering any price she would ask for it. Her desperate eyes were what only a mother understood, but the other mother's pity wasn't enough to save her because she said she had no hand in it at all.

Her little girl did all the work to make that bike her own, her mother said.

But out of pity, she went to her little artist and told her what the little boy wanted. And how much they were willing to pay for her bike.

To all of their amazement, she was willing to sell it. But to the girl's surprise, the boy jumped on her bike and was off without waiting or even saying thank you as he rode by. Although the boy's mother said what *he* should have, it bothered the little girl for a while.

But she quickly forgot his rude manner as she counted the money in her hands. Her mother was shocked by the exchange and asked her daughter, "Why did you sell your beautiful bike?" "Because he wanted it more than I do," she said. "All the fun of it is gone because I have no more space left to decorate it."

Self-Discovery – Chapter 6 – True vs. Untrue

1. **What kind of love hurts?**

    a.   parental love

    b.   love toward others

    c.   untrue love

2. **What is the dynamic that orients you to the true?**

    a.   finding what's true for you even when it's not true for others

    b.   registration with in, out, up, down, left, right aligned to the star in the void of creation

    c.   grounding yourself to the earth

3. **What does "I Am" tell you about you?**

    a.   it identifies your state of being—associative or non-associative

    b.   it identifies your structural state

    c.   it creates your experience

    d.   it tells you what you think

    e.   all of the above

4. **Why is "I am loving" a true guidance principle?**

    a. because it is primary and non-associative, it is a condition of the true self

    b. it defines the state of being that can see what is untrue

    c. it comforts a discomforting condition

    d. it can separate your feelings from what others are feeling that you may be associating with your own

    e. all of the above

5. **What is the essential meaning of delineating the 'I Am?'**

    a. delineation is the condition of your internal environment

    b. delineation is to clarify what I am

    c. delineation is to create what I am

    d. delineation identifies what is truly me

6. **Why is the boy, in the story "The Bicycle," a demonstration of the untrue?**

    a. because his mother gives him anything he wants

    b. because when he sees something someone else has that he wants, he believes it will make him happy to have it

    c. he is untrue because he shows no gratitude for what he is given

Journal Prompt – Get inspired!

In our story "The Bicycle," there are illustrations of true and untrue. Think deeply about each situation for each character. Make no assumptions by the surface or obvious and dig deep into each character's motivation.

Answer this question: Which of the characters—the bike, the girl, the boy, or the moms—suffers in their condition of untrue, and why? Hint: It's not the mothers.

the untrue condition is outside of you
the true condition stays within you

Answers: 1c, 2b, 3c, 4e, 5c, 6b

Self-Discovery

Journal

Self-Discovery

Journal

CHAPTER SEVEN

MAN VERSUS WOMAN

With every event that occurs in your life, there's always a distinction about who you should be. The next time you are part of an event, notice whether you behave in a way where people understand you, as you. Or do they understand you as a man or a woman? Ask yourself if you're presented in a room where your position is identified by your gender. If so, then you are dictated by the rules and regulations of a society that separates what is recognized for "man" from what is "woman." Because every opinion you have will be based on some condition you align to in either man or woman, even if you identify as neither or both, or some strange interpretation in-between. This condition we refer to is not physical.

THE RULES OF CONDUCT

The condition of man versus woman isn't about male and female, at least not for this chapter. This chapter is about: *What does my culture, what do my surroundings, and what does this embodiment of community around me, expect from me, as either a man or a woman?*

By social laws, unspoken or otherwise, your behavior is often dictated to—to either be listened to or to be tossed aside, because your opinion does not matter on some subject, if you're a man or a woman. Even your confidence in or knowledge of a topic may be subdued because you're a man or a woman.

NATURE: DOES IT MATE?

Life is weird when it comes to male and female because it only has one law—Does it mate? Can it make more? In the way that it mates and makes more, does it create a family, or is it some community that raises the young? As far as laws of nature for male and female, that's about it. Does it mate? Does it make another one of itself? And how will it raise that other one of itself? But that's not true for human society.

if you want to be the true you, if you want to

reach your accelerated self,

you must divorce yourself from what is man or

what is woman

NATURE VS. CULTURE

When it comes to human society, what is Man and what is Woman changes; for every decade, every century, every millennium. It changes with the ways of a culture. How man or woman is valued and what they're valued for also changes in each culture.

So, if you want to be the true you, if you want to reach your accelerated self, you must divorce yourself from what is man or what is woman, in order to be fully yourself. Think about it. How often do you go about your daily tasks, never even noticing whether you're a man or a woman? It doesn't enter your mind. It's not until you are in the company of other men or women that your behavior is somehow dictated based on those delineations of I am man, or I am woman.

I AM MAN VS. I AM WOMAN

For review, ID is the *I am* and the delineation is what follows I am. You'll automatically identify yourself by how you see yourself, in any condition, any moment, or any situation.

Delineation follows the I am. So, if you say, *I am man* or *I am woman*, then every delineation under the list of *I ams* that are man or woman are based on at least fifty percent cultural. Meaning, fifty percent of what you believe yourself to be, has been programmed in you by your culture, based on a single delineation of being man or woman.

For example, if you say you are a strong woman, *I am a strong woman,* it's perceived differently than saying *I am strong* if you are a man.

A man who says *I am strong,* is talking about his physicality; how much he can lift, pull, or bear. But a man who says *I am weak,* we assume it's about his character.

But when we say, *She is a strong woman,* we're talking about what she can bear emotionally, psychologically, or even how she holds herself in the company of men or other women. Is she strong compared to the men? That is the question of the delineation for a woman to say, *I am strong.*

A woman is also dictated to in a culture by whether she bears children. Is she a mother in her *I am?* Or not a mother in her *I am?* One day, human culture will flip that. Being a father will be of the utmost decider as to what kind of man he is.

GOOD MAN, GOOD WOMAN

How good of a father he is dictates how good of a man he is. Although that is already working in the culture, a good man is a good father, but a good father isn't always a good man. A good man is dictated by how well he treats women, how good he is to women, how good of a friend he makes of women. A good man is dictated by how women see him as a father, as a husband, as a friend.

A good woman is dictated by how well she supports her man, her children, her family. Does she support them emotionally, psychologically, financially? But how good a man he is, is how well he treats others.

A bad man treats people badly. A bad woman is just a bad mother, a bad wife, a bad daughter.

These distinctions in the delineation of the *I am* for man versus woman are all cultural—not character, not soul, not individual. They are all cultural because language around gender describes how culture sets up its society, which is based on two things.

LABOR

The first thing set up in how gender is described is about earning a living, how a society earns its living. Every stage of that earning a living determines the language around the separation of labor.

At a time when labor was purely physical, a man made more money than a woman because he could lift more, he could pull more—he was stronger.

That changes in an electronic society where intellect determines how well you advance. Labor becomes less important. Therefore, man versus woman culturally is based on intellectual competition, not physical competition.

The language around male and female is becoming more androgynous, less decided by gender. This is because competition is being equalized on intellect and not physiology. And though, man versus woman, in the male physical construct and the female physical construct, does dictate certain abilities better than the other. Meaning males are good at these things in general; females are good at these things, in general.

In individuals however, there can be intellectual compensations to what is physiologically leaning in male or female, just as the body composite either produces an offspring through it or doesn't. Hormones, glands, neurons, and brain construction all decide whether the infancy of human is incubated in a form or not. This is all related to the evolution of the species. In the evolution of a species, female contains certain abilities built in to the architected structure, which is different from male. And it's all about how male and female evolved in hunter-gatherer systems.

EVOLUTIONIZING

If hunting and gathering are no longer how humans make a living, male and female can evolve to have similar intellects, until there's a near androgynous form. This effect can minimize the potential for reproduction.

In fact, believe it or not, there are already humanoid species that have lost their ability to reproduce. They are up in the skies in ships, and have lost their worlds long ago. They have evolved out of the entire sexual reproducing system, creating a synthetic form of reproduction, which utilizes testy extraction and a test-tube incubation process.

Think about what kind of man and woman this culture creates, if there are no longer delineations based on reproduction? It would have to be a heightened, surreal capacity in each male and female. Societies can bypass all those millions of years of evolution to get to this heightened capacity. Usually, it would take an entire million years to evolve a species so distant from its relatives on the evolutionary tree that it no longer needs reproduction to make more of itself. But you can bypass that whole evolutionary branch simply by disallowing your culture to define you as a man or a woman. And yet, there's another story to reproduction entirely.

ROMANCE

That whole other story is about romance. So, let's say you fall in love with a man, a "manly" man. The best way to understand a manly man is to remain a womanly woman. You can find the highest capacity of what is woman, in order to love what is the highest capacity of that man, and that is what your soul destined to do. That's why it decided to be a man, or a woman, in this lifetime. Your soul saw from a heavenly view the power in each. Though culturally there were restraints on each, to achieve the best capacity of each, the soul knew from a heavenly view, that you could bypass the cultural dismissal of each high capacity simply by attaining your higher-self directive.

if you let anything dictate to you -
you become more of a product
of the world
than a product of your own maker

THE HIGHER-SELF DIRECTIVE

What is the directive of the higher self? It's all about: *Do not lock me in. I am more every day. I can be who I am any day, and I will be what I am today. And what I am is not dictated by what a man or a woman is, but what I am. And in that which I am, I will continuously be, regardless of the clothes that I wear, the length of my hair, whether I shave or whether I don't, whether I wear shoes with heels or shoes in flats, whether I wear a skirt or pants. I am dictated only by my capacity, not by whether I am a man or a woman, and I will see all those that I know have capacity, whether they are a man or a woman.*

Man versus woman is always a question you must ask of yourself.

Who do I become in this moment?

The higher-self directive would say that if I were a man in this moment, I would dictate to all else what we do in this moment, without care or concern for what others think. Or it would say, if I am a woman in this moment, I will hush this child in my arms without worry that I will be looked at as less than a man. I will nurture my child because of the good man I am, not because of a man they think I should be.

If you let anything dictate to you because of how you wear your skirt, your shoes, your hat, your shirt, you become more of a product of the world than a product of your own maker; the one who made you perfect as you are. Neither man nor woman, but the best of each.

The foundation of this chapter is how you delineate the *I am* based on your own character rather than on your gender.

If a woman says, *I am not worried about what people think anymore*, she's usually age 40 or over. This is because she's lived long enough to know that she could work as hard as she wants toward goals, and they can disappear in a moment. By 40, she's learned that. *I will not cut myself back for fear of what others think, nor just so others have something I've given of myself for them.*

When a man says, *I will raise my children my way*, it is because he's been pushed out of the way too many times when it comes to what he was as a child. He says, *My child, by God, will not be without the things I was without.* And he invests in his offspring and their outcome.

you are more than the urges given
to you by your hormones

DRAINED SELF AND HORMONAL DICTATES

Becoming more of the woman you are, or more of the man you are, must not be dictated by the world, nor ought it be dictated by your hormones. You are more than the urges given to you by your hormones.

If you are fully engendered into a woman, your hormones will want you to reproduce. That's why they're there. *Give me babies!* Her hormones say. *Give me babies to care for!* Everything that is in that hormonic resonance, the hormone resonance, becomes all about "caring for." That is the evolution, or the success of the evolution of the physiological form known as female, not woman mind you, but female. So that urge is biological, not individual nor soulful. It will have its own, very loud wants over the rest of you at times.

For a man, what is dictating to him is, *Let me let this sperm go! Let me have sex! Let me reproduce!* And if you're dictated by that constant drive in your hormonal structure, it will dictate your relationship with women; dictating what kind of woman you choose, and what kind of woman you wind up making mistakes with. This is because your hormones are saying who you pick, rather than the greater mind within you that will tell you very clearly, *She's not the one you want children with. She's not going to be there when times get tough.* But your hormones won't care. They just want to do it because that's why they're there; they're there to reproduce.

In a time when humans were wild, there were all the resources available, in a habitat available to this wild human. Many, many children died in the process of survival, but nature seeking redundancy was prolifically creating more, for all those that will die.

At least two or three that survive, over time they are old enough to reproduce and continue, generation after generation. If you just follow what those hormones tell you, which began as wild humans, you will eat your way out of your own habitat.

GREATNESS

Man versus woman has to do with the physical only when the physical is being dictated by a culture that needs to survive.

Beyond survival, man versus woman must be all about the spiritual, when the culture no longer supports the individual. Man, woman spiritually says, *What is the best of woman I can be? What is the best of man I can be, that is not dictated by my culture?*

You are what you are that is beyond your physical form. Your physical form is an illusion to what you are. The illusion of what you are can be buried by your physical form, or it can be the source of inspiration for your physical form.

greatness is achieved through the spirit
of what you are, not through the
form of what you are

The spirit of you is always greater and higher than the physical you. And when we say greater, we don't mean 'more than good'—we mean great as in greatness.

Greatness is achieved through the spirit of what you are, not through the form of what you are, until the spirit of what you are has a place through the form. And when the spirit of what you are has a place through the form, then the form is no longer dictating *who* you are that is present at an event, some event, whether that event is just between you and a man or a woman.

This chapter is simple and complex because you are simple and complex. The man/woman complex is cultural but the best of each is spiritual. Be what is the best of you that incorporates both into your highest capacity.

Self-Discovery – Chapter 7 – Man vs. Woman

1. **Why does being a man or a woman matter to a culture?**

    a.   division of labor

    b.   making offspring

    c.   making homes fit for raising the young

2. **How much of how you define yourself as a man or a woman is cultural?**

    a.   100%

    b.   50%

    c.   10%

3. **Why is man versus woman part of the accelerated self?**

    a.   because being a man or a woman will define what you can achieve

    b.   because to find your true self, you must not notice whether you're a man or woman

    c.   because to accelerate, you must live by the rules of a society that tells you what is a man or what is a woman

4. **What makes a culture define gender roles?**

    a.   how a culture earns its living

    b.   how a culture conducts mating rituals

    c.   how a culture defines a home

    d.   how a culture identifies romance

5. **What kind of culture evolves an androgynous form?**

    a.   intellectual

    b.   heightened surreal

    c.   hunter-gatherer

    d.   all of the above

Journal Prompt – Get inspired!

Think about the gender roles you witnessed when you were a child. What man or woman or both had expectations of you, as a child, based on being male or female? How did it influence you? How did it program how you see yourself, your potential, or the roles available to you?

you'll automatically identify yourself
by how you see yourself in any condition,
any moment, or any situation

Answers: 1a, 2b, 3b, 4a, 5a

Self-Discovery

Journal

Self-Discovery

Journal

CHAPTER EIGHT

JOY VERSUS SORROW

[Hello again, dear reader, it's Sondra here. Allow me to set the scene for you. Imagine you're standing among granite headstones, marble mausoleums, and garden benches. It's a warm, humid, Fall afternoon, in Houston, Texas. Large black crows caw over head in the tree branches, as they take flight an eerie silence settles. A gentle wind makes a shower of yellow leaves all around. We filmed the original recording for this chapter, in a century-old graveyard. And so, God begins.]

PRIORITY

One of the past times in the human mind is to begin each day with the construction of the day. *What is in my day that I must do first?* Which comes immediately after coffee, a glass of water, or a run. So, the first things you do always precede priority. Remember that, as we work through this chapter—remember the day's priority always comes after the first thing you do in the morning when you wake up.

People are buried in this graveyard, and some souls are trapped in this place. They hang around and wander through here. You may only see them at night, with special lenses, special light. And some people can see these wandering souls without any auxiliary equipment at all. Others can only sense something present—*Someone's here, but I can't see anyone.*

That's the second thing to consider as we're working through this chapter—consider presence, and the idea that it can be made aware of without a body in the course of death.

So, there's priority and what precedes priority; and there's presence even in the course of death.

SORROW

Sorrow is a condition of that which is inside. Not only is it inside, sorrow is the internal condition of an imploded state. Now, when you say, *I am sorry*, and you honestly mean that you are sorry about something, it means you regret what's been done, what's been said, how things have turned out. In that sorrow, you feel guilt for not seeing what you should have seen. In this kind of sorrow, *I'm sorry* is a head bowed and it's an internal adjustment. But that's not the type of sorrow we are talking about when it is pitted against joy.

Sorrow versus joy can come in a meaningful way or a meaningless way. It's meaningless when sorrow seems to have no meaning to it--it may have a reason but that's different from meaning. Meaningless sorrow is indeed the opposite of joy.

SOULS

People who haunt a graveyard have a body decaying underground. Sometimes that soul is hanging around its corpse because it doesn't know itself outside of a body. By this, the soul's sorrow is coming from its own death. Its sorrow is based on death.

Sorrow based on life is something you can fix. It's something you can change, something that has another outcome if you take responsibility for it. If you're sorry about how you treated someone, or an event that took place, or how things came about, it means you can do whatever is necessary to the best of your ability and change that outcome from sorrow to forgiveness.

But once the body passes, that opportunity to ask for forgiveness is lost. The opportunity is gone because the brain is no longer a functioning part of the mind. The mind is being processed instead through a sorrowful soul, a soul that has a memory of a sorry state.

Let's say this soul is a child. Because many times ghosts *are* children. They did not grow up to understand the nature of life and death. Or even the nature of heaven, God, or angels. There are many times in history where children would die often. This is why the children's prayer exists that says, "Now I lay me down to sleep, I pray the Lord my soul to keep, if I die before I wake, I pray the Lord my soul to take." The reason it exists in human memory is from haunted graveyards. The souls of children wander, looking for their parents who have long gone, who are long dead.

Theses dead children didn't know where to go. They didn't know what to do. They didn't know they would die.

Every day, people die not knowing they're going to die. They are unprepared for their death. When death comes upon you unexpectedly, for many of the dead there's shock, horror, and a confused soul that doesn't know where to go.

An untimely death is one of the most important reasons why joy is a critical condition for the soul. The soul comes to Earth in a state of joy. It's elated to suddenly be upon the Earth, delighted to be in a body having a physical experience. Because where it came from was not a physical experience. Your soul emerged into your physical state and arrived as a newborn infant.

POWERLESS

Babies cry very easily because they have no power. They can't do anything. Although a baby's mind is very active, as active as it was in its previous life, the difference now though is that mind is in a tiny body that is unable to do anything, at all!

However, what is brought to a baby by the parents and grandparents is the joy of being a baby. In that joy, the baby has those who are doing for it. And they love this baby even though they're doing everything the baby can't do for itself.

We'll tell a story to encapsulate this complex event in a soul's emergence.

ONCE UPON AN URGE

Once upon a time, in a land far away, there lived an uncontrollable urge. This wild urge lived on its own. It didn't perform. It didn't do anything. It just was. And as it was, it was always in a state of urgency. It constantly urged.

Now, the problem this urge had was that it didn't know what its urge was. Was its urge to eat, to sleep, to run, to swim, to fly? What *urge* is the urge urging to be?

And then, one day, the urge became aware of itself.

The urge said, *I am feeling an urge to eat. I am feeling an urge to cry. I am feeling an urge to defecate.* Because until the *urge* was identified, there was no self that could be identified at all—it's just urgency.

Now, this urgency lived without control. And it lived by its out-of-control urges constantly.

Until, one day, someone picked it up and made it do something it didn't want to do.

Suddenly, that urgency turned to retribution, rejection, and defiance. In the defiant state this urgency split, from a singular urge to an urge to get away, an urge to depart from the one who was not paying attention to the urge's urges.

* * *

In the story of the urge, suddenly, there was a split from *all is me* to *all is me, except this.*

There became a neurological process. The same occurred with the baby who couldn't do anything; a new process began, in the urgency split. One of, *If the one who's taken me from the thing I am urged to do, loves me, then they will do it for me. They will give me a clean diaper, give me something to eat, something to drink, they will take me out of this hot spot in the car.*

All the satisfactions of these urges—the urge to be somewhere safe, suddenly picked up and safe—every time there was satisfaction in that urgency, there went from sorrow to joy. For both the baby and the uncontrollable urge.

That joy was initially associated with someone else, a caretaker, one who was taking care of needs, taking care of urgencies. And every need became urgent to this little urge. With every urgent need that was satisfied then, joy came in the process of satisfaction.

your joy comes from you, and you have all the
responsibility to keep that joy intact

THE POWER TO MAKE JOY

So, look at yourself for a moment. Where in your life do you find urges that are dissatisfied, or unsatisfied? Where is a dissatisfied urge which you wait for someone else to satisfy? Because it's in these places in you where you'll find your sorrowful states.

And when you find satisfaction in what you have done to satisfy an urge on your own, then there is a joyous state. As long as you take care of them and do not put all that power into someone else to take care of them, simple satisfactions of an urge put you in power of your own joy.

Your joy comes from you, and you have all the responsibility to keep that joy intact.

THE PLOT IN YOUR LIFE'S STORY

We have set this chapter in a graveyard because the headstones represent an identity—someone's name, their birth, their death, the family they are a part of, whether they are a mother or a father, a daughter or a son, a grandfather or a grandmother—these conditions of a plot in the story of the life of a soul, may not mean the end for these individual souls, but it is the end of that identification, that ID, that life story.

Every life story will come to an end with either joy or sorrow. Sorrow for what did not occur in the time that life had, or joy in a long happy life, for all they got done in their time.

You can have a long, sorrowful life as well. But, if you make certain urges your responsibility, the joy of your life is held in the palm of your hand.

THE HIGHER SELF

The accelerated self, and the reason for this book and training, is all about how to engage the higher self, so that it aligns your decisions to speed up the tempo of your joy. The speed with which you make joy, every day in every way possible, must have a tempo for the ways of life to keep pace with your drive to thrive. But if the speed of which you satisfy an urge slogs through your day each day, only to find mere moments of reprieve at the end of your day, by the time you close out your week, your states of sorrow have accumulated.

LOSING LIFE FORCE

The longer it takes to satisfy an urge, the shorter your life becomes. Because sorrow squeezes the very life force that keeps the soul's position in this world. It becomes shorter because the soul identifies joy in the course of *its* realm, and its realm is eternal. By comparison, what the soul connects joy to is a mere spec of a lifetime. When an eternal experience connects to a reduced life, the soul can only perform its job in mere moments you allow the soul joy.

The soul is an organ whose only job is to bring you joy. It will show you what joy you need. But if you're constantly thinking about what work needs to be done, before you think about what joy to experience in a day, then by the end of that week you will be lost in sorrow, disengaged from the joy of the soul.

JOY AND THE SPEED OF SATISFACTION

There are ways to bring joy to the self so that you work on a faster tempo of satisfaction.

Joy is simple.

Joy doesn't need some grandiose purpose in life that you must satisfy and fulfill before you find joy. Joy every day can be found in the simplest ways.

When you are cold and you can't seem to get warm, and then you fill up a hot tub and soak in it, there is joy. Your urgency to warm up is finally satisfied. If you have a chocolate craving, and you satisfy that craving with just a little bit of chocolate, that's all you need for joy. Anything beyond that is a habit of going to chocolate when you feel sorrow.

If you lean on unhealthy satisfactions when you feel sorrow, it means you're not feeding your joy throughout the course of a day and satisfying in you that urge to be alive, the urge to live.

THE DEAD

The dead do not represent sorrow. Nor do they represent joy. The dead signify a life that has come at a beginning and then to an ending. Every beginning and ending is a period of time that you fill with either joy or sorrow.

You may think, *Well surely there's something in between. There's got to be something in between joy and sorrow. It can't be so black or white.* But unfortunately, that is the nature of every moment in your life, every thought that enters your mind. With each thought, you are either in a state of joy or a state of sorrow, and the only control you have is when you satisfy your urges.

---

an urge is not a distraction from where you are,
it's an indication of where you are

URGE OR HABIT

Let's talk about the difference between an urge and a habit now, because you may find yourself satisfying urges only to form new habits. And then, you find yourself in the middle of that habit, and it's bringing you sorrow because it's either making you fat, or it's blurring your head, or it's losing you friends.

An urge is not a distraction from where you are, it's an indication of where you are.

An urge to sleep indicates you are tired, therefore tired is where you are. But the urgency to sleep, satisfying the sleep, may be causing you problems; sleeping more than you should means you're not getting the things done you need to get done. When you're tired often, it means the satisfaction of that urgency has to be more than just sleeping.

Tiredness may need satisfaction through exercise, energy given to the body. Sometimes it needs an injection of amino acids and proteins. Sometimes the urge to sleep actually means you need to be among friends. If you've been alone too long, then there's no energy brought from the interaction you get with friends.

Satisfying joy requires that you to see beyond that simple thing, the one thing that's causing you an urge.

Unexamined urges can form a new habit. The urge to be energized for example, can create positive habits, or it can create negative habits; bad habits that keep you up late or don't let you sleep at all.

---

satisfy the urge to give up through modest,
simple decisions

TO BE OR NOT TO BE

The satisfied urge isn't just a want. It's a serious physiological aspect of life.

The urge to live is an urge to be! It's the first urge that comes through the physical form. The urge to survive gets the body through very trying times, just from the simple urge to stay alive.

On the other hand, the urge to die is the urge to give up, to stop struggling. But you can satisfy that urge to give up and stop struggling without offing yourself or dropping out of society.

Satisfy the urge to give up through modest, simple decisions.

If you're in a complex quandary about what to do about this or that, and your confusion causes stress, the way to overcome this or that is to approach it with a sense of elation, *I can't wait till this is over! It's going to be so exciting when this is over.* Looking forward to the end takes the pressure off you, in the stress of a moment. You get a reprieve by looking forward to the end. And yet, there's a backside to that coin.

If you continually work through stress by looking forward to it being over, when do you get to live? When do you get to live in that moment? When are you even present to what's happening, as it happens? That's the equivalent to watching a car screeching toward you, rather than maneuvering away, you close your eyes and wait for the inevitable. Your hands move off the wheel, leaving the end without your control.

If you project your mind into a future, which comes after an untold number of events in the middle, then you're not engaged in the events themselves.

So, the way to reduce the stress and bring joy to that moment is to look only at what's right here. Here, in the moment. Don't acknowledge the huge—*all the things I still have to do that I don't have done*—but only look at *What's next?* With the completion of each step ask, *What's next?* Then, you've simplified your mind to focus only on what's right in front of you.

Those tiny little steps at your feet are the urges you satisfy throughout the day.

Use a task list to maintain the momentum of joy. This works because there's a surge of joy with each completed task you mark off. A to-do list manages joy in time with your day. The tempo is lively and fulfilling, instead of projecting your mind beyond a single day, which is the source of stress and overwhelm, sorrow and depleted energy.

GREATNESS IS IN TINY COMPLETIONS

Try it for yourself. Notice that every single time you physically check something off of your list of things to do today, there's joy! Here's another reason not to just look forward to something being done before it's done, you miss all the things that make it a job well done.

When you rush over the step-by-steps, eager to be done, in the end, you're sorry at about how poorly you performed. Then from a meager ineffectual performance, sorrow returns.

Projection might offer momentary stress reprieve, but it adds to the growing pile of disappointment in one's self. This heap of sorrow is especially noticeable in the exact moment you have forgotten where you are.

THE URGENCIES

In the process of all the doing you do, whenever you lose your place, there's a whole lot of overwhelm to overcome. To overcome anything—disappointment, mistakes, missteps—these take inordinate amounts of energy. Add to that the overwhelm itself, which drains the energy you need to get back to 'here,' where you were before you lost your place, in the process of all the doing. The reason is that big leaping loops are dissatisfying; but small, little completions are very rewarding in each moment they occur.

Satisfying urges must be in the tiny, the very small. The smaller they are, the easier to satisfy. Joy is small. Joy is accumulative.

The more you feel joy, the greater you are; not great as in better than good, but in achievement. Greatness is achieved through tiny, little moments. Each is a successful fulfillment—an urge fulfilled.

WHEN LIFE IS HARD

When a sorry state of mind is because you're sorry that life is so hard, it means you're sorry that you wound up where you are, or it means your environment has not supported your progress in any way, so you've had to slog through your progress, pushing and pushing. That kind of life-is-so-hard sorrow means you haven't given yourself the joy of overcoming a difficult time; you don't give yourself credit for everything you've overcome.

Because joy is not only about satisfying urges, it's also about looking back and recognizing how amazing you are. How amazing YOU are!

CREATE ABUNDANCE THROUGH JOY

One last thing. We want you to remember this; remember it always.

Life only feels abundant in the joy you bring to a moment, not the joy you bring to life as a whole.

Sorrowful moments are a part of your heart. But they need not be the sum of your life—even if you've had some very sorrowful moments in your life. Even if you're in a deep well of sorrow now. It's transitional. Sorrow is just a part of you that is not able to see the greatness of you. A part of you that is buried in all the smallness of you. And that condition of all the smallness of you just happens to be a way of thinking about you. It's a way of *thinking* about you—but it is not you.

You are *not* the one who is sorrowful. You are the one with an urge to be satisfied.

Begin small, start satisfying those urges small, every day, and over time they build a joyful life.

Self-Discovery – Chapter 8 – Joy vs. Sorrow

1. **How do urges find joy?**

    a.   through finding purpose in life

    b.   through satisfaction

    c.   through someone's approval of your needs

    d.   all of the above

2. **Why does a task list bring you joy?**

    a.   because you're getting things done

    b.   because the list represents your urges

    c.   because your day goes faster

    d.   because the small act of checking things off your list creates moments of satisfaction

3. **Why is presence in the course of death important to joy or sorrow?**

    a.   because presence is the soul's experience of joy or sorrow after death

    b.   because presence is either joyful or sorrowful

    c.   because presence can be felt

    d.   both a and b

4.   **Why can an unplanned death cause confusion for the soul?**

   a.   because it doesn't know itself without a body

   b.   because it doesn't know where to go

   c.   because it identifies itself through its body

5.   **Why do some people have a sorrowful life?**

   a.   because they have no relationship with their soul

   b.   because they don't know how to bring joy to their soul

   c.   because they deny themselves moments of joy throughout the day

   d.   because they let the mind revisit up bad memories

   e.   all of the above

   f.   none of the above

Journal Prompt – Get inspired!

This writing assignment will take you a week, for making observations. Carry a notebook around with you that has a designated section just for "Shifts." These are the activities or small gestures that move you into joy. Document the instances that shift you: when you enjoy what you're doing, when you feel a lift in your mood or attitude.

Document what you're doing, when you feel yourself in your happy place. Don't bother with writing the moments of sorrow or sadness, but if you *do* notice sorrow, do something that makes the shift, and write down what that is.

If you find that all you're doing is stressful, or work-related, consider adjusting your mood or approach to those doings. What would make it more joyful? A change in your manner (how you approach it)? Or a change in environment or location? Maybe it simply requires organization and a new tactic.

As you feel that change, take note of what made the shift. The goal is to list as many activities as possible, that offer new attitudes or internal adjustments from sorrow to joy.

Answers: 1b, 2d, 3d, 4b, 5e

Journal

Self-Discovery

Journal

CHAPTER NINE

ABUNDANCE VERSUS LACK

OPENINGS

Every opening that has an awakening is filled with all kinds of shifts. There's a shift in the right, a shift in the left, a shift in the up, and a shift in the down; the shifts are internal, in the psychosomatic—the soma of being.

The psychosomatic is your psychology in the soma, the psychology that affects the soma; the soma is the parts of an organism, except the reproductive cells.

So, an awakening that has an opening occurs inside your being—in your physiology and psychology. An opening is psychosomatic.

INSIDE OUTSIDE IN

Now, any time there is an opening in the psychosomatic, it filters through your entire being, and into the condition of your mind. As your mind is interacting with your outside (what's happening), that opening begins to change or alter the edges of your reality—becoming a more surreal reality.

This is how you experience waking up from sleep. The opening hovers in some kind of in-between phase of the unconscious state moving to a conscious one.

Waking up means the sleep dimension slowly diminishes away, taking you to a different dimension. As you wake up, you're pulling up and out through this opening; through an *open*.

Remember when we talked about apertures? In chapter three, we said a mind that's looking for something will cause the aperture of the soul to open up.

ZERO POINT

Apertures open. Such as an aperture of the soul. Like the aperture of a camera, it opens to allow light in. This opening occurs in the median range, between unconscious and being physically awake. In that middle range between physically at rest and awake, and physically at sleep, or unconscious, there is a plateau, or an opening to each. This opening has a very clear zero point. A zero point where you are neither awake nor asleep.

If we assign numbers to this range, five below the decimal point for stages of falling asleep (-5, -4, -3, -2, -1) into states of waking up (+1, +2, +3, +4, +5) we see clearly where the zero point sits, between plus and minus one.

Keep that in mind. Because we'll discuss how the range of unconscious to conscious has an opening in both directions.

GOD AND THE PSYCHE

Sondra opens her psyche to our being; we refer to ourselves as God. A word derived from the good. The All that is good. All that is all, and all that has become the good. Because the All that has become the good—and therefore called God of the good—that condition has had a change. It separated from the condition of not good, or as some call evil, but we say it is the complete opposite of love. Evil is completely devoid of love.

There is a void that is love. It is a void. And contained within that void is soul and spirit that is love. If you imagine a sphere, the space within the hollow of it is a void. When a door is open, there's void within its open space.

And within the void that is love, there is the way.

The historical figure, Jesus, is a story that involves the condition of the Christ. The Christ is that all-love void that is peace. It's why he's known as the Prince of Peace, the bringer of the way, the teacher of the way.

I am the way, the truth, and the life, no one goes to the Father, except through me. What he meant is that no one can tell him who is his God. Not the common laws of religion or government, because his *highest* authority is God within him. He was saying, *Nothing outside of me can dictate to me what is my God. My God is within me. My God is me.* "The kingdom of God is within you!" he proclaimed.

SYMBOLS OF OPENINGS

Sondra wears a bracelet with a symbol of her faith. It's a snowflake, but its shape reminds her of the Christmas star. As we've discussed, it's a symbol in most dominant faiths—the Star of David, the star in the symbol of Islam, and the diamond on the top of the Om. They also represent another opening, an opening in the void of creation.

Openings occur between two phases. And in our teaching today, these phases are in the psyche. The phase is one dimension that opens to another phase or dimension. In the opening is a surreal in-between.

The surreal in-between is called the zero point, it's the point between two phases, two dimensions.

And there are percentages of awareness, in each phase, where the two phases blur between each other, they bleed *into* each other. You've noticed this phenomenon when you've incorporated a sound or something happening outside of you while you slept. Therefore, your dream occurs in the same dimension as where your ears heard the sound. That is a void; a void in space between two dimensions.

BETWEEN TWO WORLDS

We're talking about opening, and we're talking about layers or levels of awareness based on that opening, and what direction of that opening you are moving into. And we also said that at about -5 to -1, as you're waking up into your own conscious state, into your three-dimensional form, you're still partially within the unconscious, and the effect is that you're having a surreal experience.

It's very real, but a there's bleed-through of some dimension of the unconscious. There's only one thing that separates these two realms: the brain.

If you were not in a body, in a brain processing the mind, you would be un-here. There may be some aspect of you here, if you have a body and a brain, but it's not functioning in the way of keeping you in a three-dimensional construct, in the way of being in a full, physical form.

The true you actually lives somewhere in-between; in the zero point. What's amazing is that in the zero point, your exterior is not physical. It is not in a physical domain because in the zero-point plateau, where you ultimately live, all is perceived, but it's your brain telling you what's real.

So, the exterior of you is in a non-physical dimension, which is a different part of you. It's a different part of you but is still you. Here's a fairly simple way to understand a complex reality you're in.

YOU-AT-HOME VS. YOU-AT-WORK

Imagine a similar construct where there is the you-at-work and the you-at-home; the you-with-your-family and the you-with-your-coworkers; the you-with-a-lover and the you-with-a-partner-at-work. Those are separations of being. They're about how you show up in your appearance; how you appear, how you show up, how you behave, what you wear, your demeanor, and your presence.

When a window appears in that awareness, a separation opening forms. It may occur as soon as you get up in the morning, drink your coffee, and get on the road or get on your computer.

It's that moment when you are no longer the other you. You are the you-at-home then the you-at-work. You change.

Your language changes because it's full of the jargon of your job. Your dispensation of information changes. You try to be as efficient as possible in how you communicate, and how you are communicated to, when you are at work. At home, there's a lot of feeling, so much feeling that you don't always have to communicate everything you need. The people you are around most often can read between the lines of things you say, or just read your body language, to know when you are ready or not ready for a fight, or ready or not ready for what's next.

This is all preliminary information we're giving you to get into your mind, this idea that there are conditions in you that change based on your environment. Your bed environment has a range, your work environment has a range. In the zero-point range, there is a crossover. The opening from one aspect of you to another contains a blend in the surreal.

Let's say at work, someone brings in a personal problem or situation, and it's something you never saw about them before. Maybe they have a weakness for a beloved or a need to be with their children or wife more, otherwise they must quit and find another job. You're seeing in that person, the part of them that lives somewhere under here; the here they are at work. You're seeing their ranges change in the up and down of their at-home self.

Maybe when you see that aspect of them in a work environment, there is a discomfort that occurs, because suddenly you are out of your category box of being.

To bring your mind back to the topic of this chapter, on abundance versus lack, whom you are being at any point of your being is determined only by the opening—what you are open to; open to receiving.

THE CHANGE WITHIN

Now, let's look at the mind for a moment. Remember our teeny, tiny little mollusk whose only job was to breathe in and breathe out? He breathed in cold water, and he breathed out warm water. The changes occurred within him. The dirtier the water, the more effort he makes, breathing in and breathing out, because his filter gets caught up by his environment.

That's how we symbolize the mind. The muddy water represents emotion brought to the function of the job being performed by breathing in and breathing out. In that clog of learning, the effort to filter properly also clogged up the filter, so that anything that came in thereafter was affected by the filter, and the filter was already clogged from the dirty water in the first place.

We also said bad memories should remain buried. Any attempt to kick up that mud alters the filter of what you breathe in, what's coming into your life, and what you're learning about yourself and your environment. Just muddies it up.

Some of that mud needs to stay undisturbed. Do not dig up your own grave because abundance versus lack are two sides of a range.

ABUNDANCE RANGE VS. LACK RANGE

In abundance versus lack, there's negative five to one, and positive one to five.

Lack is the result of the wrong filter.

Abundance says there's always opportunity, there's always a way. You could be at some different level of that abundance. You might be at level one.

And instead of being surreal, like between asleep and awake, zero point in lack and abundance is all about choice. What do you choose to live in? Do you choose to live in and breathe in the past, where you had nothing? Or breathe in the present? The present indeed shows you that you have something, if you were to count all the somethings you have.

And not just things, although it can be very helpful when you're feeling a sense of lack in your financial matters, that you list all the things that you have, in things. *I have a roof over my head. I have shoes in the closet. I have a car. I have a bed.* When you list all the things you have, you feel better. So, by the time you go to sleep, you feel peaceful, after listing off everything you have. And that is the goal, right?

If you're in a state of lack, the goal is to reach the state of abundance. The state of abundance is only reached through gratitude for where you are.

Gratitude is essential for peace, because you *could* focus on and list off, all the things you don't have, and suddenly you're in negative five. But when you start listing all the things you do have, you're in the right range for abundance. And one of those things you have is a mind!

ABUNDANCE THROUGH THE MIND

That mind has access to a greater mind, because the realm of God is simply made up of one thing—mind; mind within mind, within mind, within mind, and so on. Every layer of the mind can communicate with every other layer of the mind that's beyond you, so the aperture that opens in the unconscious, which goes bi-directionally, can be served in the mind, and therein has all the information you need, about how to manage lack and bring forth abundance, it is all at your behest.

We're going to take you into the realm of abundance in a story right now, so that you really understand what we mean by abundance. Humans think that abundance means you don't have a care in the world, that all of your needs are satisfied, all of your needs are met, and you have more than enough—more than enough love, more than enough money, more than enough real estate, more than enough beauty, more than enough man, more than enough woman, *la, ti da, ti da, ti da, ti da*. These are the things that abundance means to humans.

If you learn what abundance means to God, and what abundance means to the great believer—the you that believes in greatness, you that *is* your greatness—then you'll find what makes you great. This is what abundance means to that level of greatness in you; there's zero-point open to greatness, and then there's below zero, not so great. Your choice.

ONCE UPON A PRIDE

Once upon a time, in a land far away, there lived an elephant. That elephant stayed alone most of the time, because in the rules of the pride, male elephants are too dominating and frightening to the females and offspring. So, they are sent off on their own to maintain the circle of the territory.

This one elephant had been in the territorial scope for a long time—20 years. And he started to get tired. He couldn't do his job anymore. He couldn't walk for long travels. He couldn't ever find enough water. He couldn't ever find enough food. It seemed as if not only his habitat was shrinking, but his desire for life was shrinking. So, he did something elephants don't normally do—he hid.

Elephants think hiding is cowardly, and it's against the rules of the community to disappear from the territorial governance. This is because the little ones stay safe over long distances by the sound of an elephant warning of predators in the area or alerting to where there is water.

That is a dependable elephant, who is not only dependable to the pride, but dependable to his role in the pride. If he is not dependable in the role of his pride, then he knows that's the end of his life in the pride. And he was welcoming that.

For the first time, he welcomed the end. Before, he had fought against it. He played his role as best he could, but finally, after 20 years, he felt too alone.

One day, as he's laying in the grass, he's actually feeling happy for the first time, because he's divorced himself from his role. He's divorced himself from the obligation of the pride, and he has found his perfect spot.

But one day, while sleeping in pure joy, a juvenile bull elephant comes upon him and nudges him with his tusks. When the big old elephant awoke, he saw this young elephant, and thought he was looking at himself. This elephant looked so much like him, he thought he was looking at himself because he had just been startled awake from his deep, deep sleep. When he noticed that, and he couldn't understand the surreal picture he was seeing, and he was trying to shake it off, and as he shook his head, this juvenile was mimicking his behavior only because he'd never seen a big old male bull before. He had heard they were out there but had never seen one.

When the big old elephant shook it off and realized this was a young elephant before him, he stood up. The young elephant was startled by his size, startled by his massiveness. Even though he was old, he had not lost his massiveness. When the juvenile looked at him, he shook his head and he said, *Will I be as big as you, someday?*

Now, the big old elephant thought for sure he had been busted. He felt like he should run, because if they come and find him, they will destroy him, he thought. This is because he's breaking the rules of his society. But he decided not to be afraid, because he kind of liked this young juvenile, and he could tell he had something he could teach him so that he did a good job. Like he had done for 20 years.

So he said to the young juvenile, *Not only will you get as big as me, you will be able to tour the whole territory, and in your tour of the whole territory, you might one day save the pride from great danger, just like I did.*

And the juvenile said, *Aww, man. That's not what I want to do. I don't want to spend my life just like you.*

The old elephant, now feeling somewhat discouraged that this young elephant did not want to carry on the pride, also found himself feeling the same way.

So, he said, *Well, let me take you down the tour that I did for 20 years, and let's just talk, and maybe you'll change your mind. If nothing else, you'll give me someone to talk to, and someone to teach before I die, all the things I've learned.*

And the young juvenile was so excited about that. He thought that was the best idea he'd heard for weeks. And so, the two of them went on a journey of discovery, together.

* * *

The old elephant represents the part of you that is tired and lonely sometimes. This is where nothing ever seems to go exactly the way you decide, but someone else decides. Where someone else decides for you how you spend your day, your work life, and you never get anything your way.

The young juvenile represents the part of you that is afraid of hard work and would rather cut corners or do something else, anything else but your job, your obligations. This young you just needs a conversation with the old you. This is so the old you trains the young you all the ins and outs, the ups and downs, and the side to sides.

TO WHERE WITH ALL YOU

As that training occurs, the young you who has all the wherewithal to see the bigger picture, and in that bigger picture, organize the information from the big old experienced you.

You don't have to tour the countryside to find out the best places to stand and watch for predators, because you have the learning coming to you. The big elephant also represents the bigger mind, the one that has already scoped it out long before you were even out, ready to learn, ready to be in a place to learn something new. Abundance means all you need is at your disposal. It doesn't mean that all you want is available to you. It means all you need is right there in front of you. Lack is when you don't know that all you need is right there in front of you, or right there within you.

Now, we hope this whole book generates progressive questions, and in each progressive question, there is an answer that goes deeper in your knowing.

Thank you for joining us on your journey to an accelerated self. Be well, be strong, and stay abundant.

Self-Discovery – Chapter 9 – Abundance vs. Lack

1.   **What does the zero point have to do with lack and abundance?**

     a.   it's the point where you choose between states in the mind

     b.   it's the point at which you own nothing

     c.   it's the point where all is unknown to you

     d.   it's where you can't decide what you want

2.   **Where does abundance require you to know your capacity?**

     a.   in the present

     b.   in the past

     c.   in gratitude for where you are

     d.   in the future

3.   **Why does gratitude for where you are bring you toward abundant states?**

     a.   because it brings peace

     b.   because the past is not dictating your state of mind

     c.   because your mind is focused on what you have over what you don't

     d.   because abundance means that all you need is available to you

     e.   all of the above

4.   **What is the zero point?**

    a.   a void

    b.   it's where the true self resides

    c.   an opening between two opposing dimensions in the mind

    d.   all of the above

5.   **Why is lack an illusion?**

    a.   because it identifies your state of being

    b.   because it means all possibilities are unavailable to you

    c.   because it robs you of reality

    d.   because it alters your reality

6.   **How does the story of the elephants teach you abundance?**

    a.   it teaches that abundance means you don't need to participate in your obligations

    b.   it teaches abundance is about shirking your responsibilities

    c.   it teaches that abundance means to allow someone else to takeover your duties

    d.   it teaches that abundance is achieved in a relationship with the old experienced you and the young student in you learning something new

Journal Prompt – Get inspired!

It's time to tell your story of accomplishment, with as many descriptions as possible. Think of a time when you worked hard on something. You felt proud when it was finished. What was that? Why was it important to you?

- While working on it, did you look forward to being done? Or focus on each step along the way? How did that affect the outcome?

- What challenges did you face? How did you overcome them? Did you ever feel like giving up somewhere in the middle? What made you persevere?

- When it was done, how did you feel? What were the accomplishments along the way? Was it the thing you finished or that you completed it which felt like an accomplishment?

- What would you have done differently? And have you taken those lessons to other accomplishments? How so?

Answers: 1a, 2c, 3e, 4d, 5b, 6d

Self-Discovery

Extra Credit Work

---

every opening that has an awakening is filled
with all kinds of shifts

What that first line from the chapter means is that the awakening you have into abundance is going to shift you from a state of lack or want. Which in turn means you either shift from wanting to not wanting, or you arrange what it takes to satisfy your wants. In that awakening, you'll shift in, out, up, down, left, and right.

From the *in*, you are working on your investment in the want. The *out* is what is outside of you to satisfy the want. From the *down* you establish where you stand. From the *up* you're entering the mind of the want. From the *left* is one choice, the *right* has another choice.

These shifts occur through the soma—they are psychosomatic.

Write about something you lack or want. Be specific, no generalities. You don't want money or security, you want to pay for something, or save a certain amount by a certain age. Come at it from a state of lack and move from the middle point, or zero-point in your mind, and explore the shifts. Write about that and find the abundant thought. Explore what awakens in you, and what is shifting.

Self-Discovery

Journal

Self-Discovery

Journal

Self-Discovery

Journal

Other Works Available

What to Do When You're Dead:
A Former Atheist Interviews the Source of Infinite Being

The Accelerated Self Program
https://grow.sondrasneed.com

Source Dialogues:
The Miracle Mechanism of Manifestation
Gary Springfield with Sondra Sneed -- transcripts
from the powerful soul readings of a 40-year
meditation instructor.

ABOUT
SONDRA SNEED

Sondra Sneed is an expert on trance communication with Universal Consciousness, which she calls God and Source. She facilitates private sessions for clients and groups with students for psychic therapy, intuition training, decision clarity, soul healing, and spiritual coaching. This work cultivates self-revelation and mind mastery. Sondra is the author of *What to Do When You're Dead* and creator of *The Accelerated Self Program*, which guides those who seek a deeper understanding of themselves and their capacity for greatness.

Having conducted more than 5,000 readings, Sondra has helped countless individuals overcome despair and loneliness, stuck potential, and guides them toward self-love and revelation. Exploring what's behind thoughts, feelings, and behaviors she also reveals insights into spiritual phenomena such as cohabitant souls, interior doorways to other dimensions, and parallel universes.

In addition to her private practice, Sondra shares Source wisdom through her on-stage performances called "Source Talks," and in her blog, radio appearances, podcasts, and a bi-annual column in *Texas Weddings* magazine.

Counting among her achievements, Sondra stood out from 3,000 worldwide applicants in a study by the Institute of Noetic Sciences (IONS), for her ability to access higher realms of consciousness. This earned a spot among twelve international finalists in a fieldwork project initiated by IONS director of research, Dr. Helena Wahbeh, author of *The Science of Channeling*. Sondra's work continues to push boundaries in the exploration of higher consciousness.

Her mission is to connect people with their higher selves for lasting transformation, by reorienting them to their essential nature. If you're ready to experience profound insight and shift your life, visit her website at https://sondrasneed.com to book a session with Source today.